STORYTELLING FOR LEADERS

Stories matter. Written by renowned psychoanalyst, leadership scholar, and executive coach, Manfred Kets de Vries, this book uncovers, explains, and captures the power and art of storytelling at work and in life, and how it can be applied in organizations to powerful effect.

Our talent in telling stories makes us more effective. When we talk about events, characters, actions, themes, feelings, and ideas, storytelling is a way to communicate our message. The stories we tell inform, influence, entertain, and shape our lives and those of other people. Using an engaging and storytelling style throughout, the book explores the important role of storytelling, with a particular focus on how it is one of the most important ways to develop leadership skills. Not only does this book present a clear method for improving our storytelling skills, it also explores themes such as the tendency of some people not to live up to their full potential, why people assume an attitude of helplessness, the effects of adversity on human development, why people behave stupidly, the psychological dynamics which affect influencers, the role of sexuality in career management, and what needs to be done to have a fulfilling life.

The book is perfect for organizational leaders looking to develop their understanding and skills in the art of storytelling, thereby increasing their effectiveness in positive and powerful ways.

Manfred F. R. Kets de Vries is the Distinguished Clinical Professor of Leadership Development and Organizational Change at INSEAD and was the Founder of INSEAD's Global Leadership Center. *The Financial Times*, *Wirtschaftswoche*, *Le Capital*, *El Pais*, and *The Economist* have rated him among the world's leading management thinkers. As a global consultant in leadership development, his clients have included many of the world's most important global organizations. He is the author of more than 50 books, hundreds of articles, and the recipient of numerous awards, including four honorary doctorates. He is also the Chairman of the Kets de Vries Institute (KDVI), a boutique leadership development consulting firm.

STORYTELLING FOR LEADERS

Tales of Sorrow and Love

Manfred F. R. Kets de Vries

Routledge
Taylor & Francis Group

LONDON AND NEW YORK

Designed cover image: "Meal of the Fool" by Micha Lobi. Copyright Kunsthandel Natalia Riedl München, natascha.bp@mail.ru

First published 2025
by Routledge
4 Park Square, Milton Park, Abingdon, Oxon OX14 4RN

and by Routledge
605 Third Avenue, New York, NY 10158

Routledge is an imprint of the Taylor & Francis Group, an informa business

British Library Cataloguing-in-Publication Data
A catalogue record for this book is available from the British Library

ISBN: 9781032833569 (hbk)
ISBN: 9781032815619 (pbk)
ISBN: 9781003508939 (ebk)

DOI: 10.4324/9781003508939

Typeset in Garamond and Scala Sans
by Apex CoVantage, LLC

CONTENTS

ABOUT THE AUTHOR

Manfred F. R. Kets de Vries brings a different view to the much-studied subjects of organizational dynamics, leadership, executive coaching, and psychotherapy. Bringing to bear his knowledge and experience of economics (Econ. Drs., University of Amsterdam), management (ITP, MBA, and DBA, Harvard Business School), and psychoanalysis (Membership Canadian Psychoanalytic Society, Paris Psychoanalytic Society, and the International Psychoanalytic Association), he explores individual and societal existential dilemmas in depth.

The Distinguished Clinical Professor of Leadership Development and Organizational Change at INSEAD, he is the Founder of INSEAD's Executive Master Program in Change Management. He has been a pioneer in team coaching as an intervention method to help organizations and people change. As an educator, he has received INSEAD's distinguished MBA teacher award six times. He has held professorships at McGill University, the École des Hautes Études Commerciales, Montreal, and the Harvard Business School. He is also a distinguished visiting professor at the European School for Management and Technology (ESMT), Berlin. He has lectured at management institutions around the world. *The Financial Times*, *Le Capital*, *Wirtschaftswoche*, and *The Economist* have rated Kets de Vries among the world's leading management thinkers and among the most influential contributors to human resource management.

Kets de Vries is the author, co-author, or editor of more than 50 books, including *The Neurotic Organization, Power and the Corporate Mind, Organizational Paradoxes, Struggling with the Demon: Perspectives on Individual and Organizational Irrationality, Handbook of Character Studies, The Irrational Executive, Leaders, Fools and Impostors, Life and Death in the Executive Fast Lane, Prisoners of Leadership, The Leadership Mystique, The Happiness Equation, Are Leaders Born or Are They Made? The Case of Alexander the Great, The New Russian Business Elite, Leadership by Terror: Finding Shaka Zulu in the Attic, The Leader on the Couch, Coach and Couch, The Family Business on the Couch, Sex, Money, Happiness, and Death: The Quest for Authenticity, Reflections on Leadership and Character, Reflections on Leadership and Career, Reflections on Organizations, The Coaching Kaleidoscope, The Hedgehog Effect: The Secrets of High Performance Teams, Mindful Leadership Coaching: Journeys into the Interior, You Will Meet a Tall Dark Stranger: Executive Coaching Challenges, Telling Fairy Tales in the Boardroom: How to Make Sure Your Organization Lives Happily Ever After, Riding the Leadership Roller Coaster: A Psychological Observer's Guide, Down the Rabbit Hole of Leadership: Leadership Pathology of Everyday Life, The CEO Whisperer: Meditations on Leadership, Life and Change, Quo Vadis: The Existential Challenges of Leaders, Leadership Unhinged: Essays on the Ugly, the Bad, and the Weird, Leading Wisely: Becoming a Reflective Leader in Turbulent Times, The Daily Perils of Executive Life: How to Survive When Dancing on Quicksand, The Path to Authentic Leadership: Dancing with the Ouroboros, A Life Well Lived: Dialogues with a Kabouter,* and *The Darker Side of Leadership: Pythons Devouring Crocodiles.* He has designed a number of 360-degree feedback instruments, including the widely used *Global Executive Leadership Mirror, Global Executive Leadership Inventory,* and the *Organizational Culture Audit.*

In addition, Kets de Vries has published more than 400 academic papers as chapters in books and as articles. He has also written more than 100 case studies, including seven that received the Best Case of the Year award. He has written hundreds of mini-articles (blogs) for the *Harvard Business Review, INSEAD Knowledge,* and other digital outlets. He is also a regular writer for various other magazines. His work has been featured in such publications as *The New York Times, The Wall Street Journal, The Los Angeles Times, Fortune, Business Week, The Economist, The Financial Times, The Straits Times, The New Statesman, The Harvard Business Review, Le Figaro, El Pais,* and *Het Financieele Dagblad.* His books and articles have been translated into more than 30 languages.

Kets de Vries is a member of 17 editorial boards, is a Fellow of the Academy of Management, and is on the board of various charitable organizations. He is also a founding member of the International Society for the Psychoanalytic Study of Organizations (ISPSO), which has honored him as a lifetime member. Kets de Vries is also the first non-US recipient of the International Leadership

Association Lifetime Achievement Award for his contributions to leadership research and development and has received a Lifetime Achievement Award from Germany for his advancement of executive education. The American Psychological Association has honored him with the Harry and Miriam Levinson Award for his contributions to Organizational Consultation. He is also the recipient of the Freud Memorial Award for his work to further the interface between management and psychoanalysis. In addition, he has received the Vision of Excellence Award from the Harvard Institute of Coaching. Kets de Vries is the first beneficiary of INSEAD's Dominique Héau Award for Inspiring Educational Excellence. He has been honored with four honorary doctorates. The Dutch government has made him an Officer in the Order of Oranje Nassau.

Kets de Vries works as a consultant on organizational design/ transformation and strategic human resource management for companies worldwide. As an educator and consultant, he has worked in more than 40 countries. In his role as a consultant, he is also the founder-chairman of the Kets de Vries Institute (KDVI), a boutique global strategic leadership development consulting firm with associates worldwide (www.kdvi.com).

On a very different note, Kets de Vries was the first fly fisherman in Outer Mongolia (at the time, becoming the world record holder of the Siberian hucho taimen trout). He is a member of New York's Explorers Club. In his spare time, he can be found in the rainforests or savannas of Central and Southern Africa, the Siberian taiga, the Ussuri Krai, Kamchatka, the Pamir Mountains, the Altai Mountains, Arnhemland, or within the Arctic Circle.

Website: www.kdvi.com

INTRODUCTION

Curiosity concerning things which one would rather not know is a human weakness.

—Molière

Tell me the facts and I'll learn. Tell me the truth and I'll believe. But tell me a story and it will live in my heart forever.

—Native American Proverb

No, no! The adventures first, explanations take such a dreadful time.

—Lewis Carroll

In Molière's five-act comedy-ballet *Le Bourgeois gentilhomme* (translated as *The Bourgeois Gentleman*), the foolish protagonist, Monsieur Jourdain, is delighted to learn during a philosophy lesson that he had been speaking prose all his life without realizing that he was doing so. Of course, looking at the play, the question remained whether he understood the importance of speaking prose. But like all of us, he had gone through life telling stories. In that respect, even though we may not always realize how important our efforts at storytelling tend to be, we are very much like Monsieur Jourdain. In fact, if we take a hard look at what we are doing, storytelling is taking much of our time. "Here's the story" is the way many of our conversations seem to start. We share stories with others more often than we may realize.

This book is a collection of essays that center around storytelling. While reading these essays, it may dawn on you that storytelling as an activity has made us very much who we are. From the time humans were able to use language, storytelling has come to the fore. It is a form of interacting with each other that has preoccupied all of us from a very young age. On a daily basis, when you talk about events, characters, actions, themes, feelings, and ideas, storytelling is a way to communicate your message. And, if you have a good story to tell, it will create genuine emotions and behavioral responses. In fact, the stories you tell will inform, influence, entertain, and shape the lives of both yourself and other people. You know what you know by telling and listening to stories. As such, it is fair to say that stories are the common currency of humanity. We all live within a network of stories. It is the way we build connections. It is the way we come to understand others. And, what's more, stories can change our lives. No wonder, given the power of storytelling, that as a species we are so addicted to them. And like addicts who cannot do without their fix, stories will never leave us. Even as you sleep, in your dreams, you are telling yourself stories. And even though we may be called *Homo sapiens*, a better description may be *Homo narratus*.

The stories you tell will inform, influence, entertain, and shape the lives of both yourself and other people.

Humans have always been storytelling animals and the oral tradition is humanity's oldest form of communication. The ability to tell stories has given our species an evolutionary advantage. Through stories, our ancestors were able to codify and communicate information important for survival. Most likely, our species would not have been able to survive without our unique ability to form networks for social cooperation—interactive networks put into place through storytelling. Stories were a means to transmit cultural values, strengthen our sense of community, and create hope for the future. Therefore, it is fair to say that humans evolved by listening to each other's stories. Without stories, there would be no nations, no culture, and no civilization. In fact, storytelling is the most powerful way to create ideas in the world that we live in. Stories determine how we think. Storytelling helps us to create shared social values, to create meaning. And through stories you learn how things work, how you make decisions (and justify them), how you can persuade others, and how you understand your place in the world. In effect, storytelling is one of the most unifying characteristics of humankind, central to human existence, and an activity that takes place in every known culture throughout the world.

Storytelling was the method of education long before education was formalized. It has always been a timeless link to ancient traditions, legends, archetypes, myths, and symbols. By studying cave paintings and other artifacts, it is fair to say that storytelling may have started in the prehistory of *Homo sapiens*. From these archaic times, onwards to the bards of Greek and Roman times, to the minstrels and troubadours of the Middle Ages, to the latest Hollywood blockbuster movies, humans have always been prepared to tell and listen to stories.

What's more, stories help you to find a degree of predictability and order in a world that's often extremely unpredictable. Stories—given their narrative structure—may help you imagine that you can have a modicum of control over your life. After all, you know that in a story's narrative, resolution follows conflict and that, eventually, there might be a safety net. Hence, given the way stories are structured, they can be used to make sense of your life in a world that often defies logic. Through storytelling you may come to see specific patterns among all the chaos and see meaning where there is randomness. They could help you to make sense out of otherwise puzzling or random events. Essentially, through your exposure to stories, the world you live in can become more comprehensible.

When you listen to a compelling story, it can sometimes feel that the storyteller is putting a spell on you. Spellbound, listening to what the person has to say, you come to recognize yourself in the story. You will be transported to another place or time, making the story even more personal. Soon, if the magic of the story is working, what is narrated will cause you to develop feelings, thoughts, opinions, and ideas that tend to align with those of the person telling the story. And, as you continue to become enchanted by the story that is being told, you will share the emotions that the story evokes, such as happiness, disgust, anger, sadness, anxiety, fear, and surprise. Thus, by simply telling a story, storytellers are able to plant ideas, thoughts, and emotions into your brain, making you share their grief, joy, and hardships. And, thus, through listening and telling stories, you learn about compassion, empathy, tolerance, and respect. In addition, you also learn about the darker side of humanity.

Stories are the common currency of humanity.

Hence, stories create a timeless link to other people's lives and experiences, the storyteller's words influencing the brain activity of their listeners. And these emotional dynamics can be influential. They can change the way you think and even behave. It is thus no wonder that stories have long been used to inform people about viewpoints beyond their own. Storytelling has always been the way to create interpersonal connections and influence group behavior.

In addition, stories will tap into your creative spirit. You may, through listening to someone's stories and experiencing the lives of other people from a completely different perspective, be able to explore the core of creativity. Given what you hear, it may stretch your imagination, encouraging you to explore different ways of thinking. In fact, the stories you listen to could help engage the right side of your brain, thereby triggering your imagination. Tapping into this well of creativity can perhaps become a source for self-discovery, the spark that can help you to reinvent yourself.

The art of storytelling could also improve your memory. Stories can be compared to memory aids, instruction manuals, and moral compasses. They can help you to structure vast quantities of information. As you may have discovered over and over again, you will remember information when it is woven into narratives substantially more than when you listen to facts alone. Consequently, your vocabulary, comprehension, sequencing skills, memory, and creativity will all grow when you tell, and listen to, stories. Once a compelling story has been told or listened to, it will be hard to escape that story's narrative framework.

Furthermore, stories can even shape your future. If you tell yourself a story wherein you can achieve this or that desired outcome, master this or that skill, the confidence that comes from believing this version of the story could turn into a self-fulfilling prophecy. Influenced by what you have learned, you may be able to acquire the competences needed to achieve whatever you would like to accomplish. In that respect, stories can become a great way of looking into the future—of predicting, of planning, and of succeeding. Every success story could turn into a lesson of how you can succeed. That is, a good story can often help dislodge an unhelpful one. The right story, told under the right conditions, can have the power to reframe events in an emotionally more positive light, in a way that no number of rational facts would ever be able to do.

Thus, listening to stories of struggle that turn out well may give you the hope that you too can also be successful in similar activities. Life stories in which you can find redemptive meaning in their messages about past challenges and ways of dealing with adversity—the kinds of life stories with ideas that include agency, exploration, or more open mindedness—become an example that you may be inclined to follow. It is these kinds of stories from which you can learn—stories that can guide you in how to deal with future challenges. Therefore, if you want to change your life, you need to change your story.

If you want to change your life, you need to change your story.

As is the case with all intervention methods, however, it needs to be said that storytelling can be used for good or bad. Demagogues have always been familiar with how stories can influence their listeners. While telling stories of hatred, they will make their followers miserable, destroying their lives.

Our challenge, then, is to create the kinds of stories that contribute to more fulfilling lives.

Hopefully, by reflecting on the stories presented in this book of essays, you will come to understand better what it means to be human. Moreover, it is my aim that by reading this collection of essays, while reflecting on your own story, you will feel more alive. After all, the greatest creation all of us have is our own life story. As the Danish writer Isak Dinesen once said, "All sorrows can be borne if you put them into a story or tell a story about them."[1]

As must have become clear by now, this book is an invitation to be more attuned to the telling and listening to stories—and to become more skilled in making sense of your own story. In that respect, storytelling may be looked at as the royal road to self-knowledge. In addition, for the sake of your mental health it will also be important that you own your own story—that you don't run away from it, whatever shadows you may encounter. And, as I also try to point out in these essays, the purpose of a storyteller is not to tell you *how* to think but to give you questions to think *about*. Stories need to become the engines of your imagination. Through stories you may be able to make sense of situations in your life that often seem to defy any logic.

NOTE

[1] Bent Mohn (3 November 1957). "A Talk with Isak Dinesen." *New York Times*.

1

BEING A STORYTELLER

Gilgamish, why runnest thou, (inasmuch as) the life which thou seekest,
Thou canst not find? (For) the gods, in their (first) creation of mortals,
Death allotted to man, (but) life they retain'd in their keeping.
Gilgamish, full be thy belly, Each day and night be thou merry, (and) daily
keep holiday revel,
Each day and night do thou dance and rejoice; (and) fresh be thy raiment,
(Aye), let thy head be clean washen, (and) bathe thyself in the water,
Cherish the little one holding thy hand;
be thy spouse in thy bosom Happy—(for) this is the dower [of man].
                                                        —The Epic of Gilgamesh

Humans have been telling stories since the dawn of time. Although the oldest recorded written story, *The Epic of Gilgamesh*, was probably put together around 2700 BCE, storytelling is considered to have a much earlier history. From the time *Homo sapiens* began to use language, storytelling had to follow. Telling stories has been one of the most unifying elements of humankind, is central to human existence, and takes place in every known culture in the world.

DOI: 10.4324/9781003508939-1

Historically, prior to the written word, storytelling would have been *the* transgenerational way to pass along knowledge and values. Cultures around the world have used and still use stories to share their histories, to present cautionary tales, and to educate their children. Stories can be considered timeless links to ancient traditions, legends, archetypes, myths, and symbols. They can engage you through their emotional content, eliciting in you the feelings of being mad, sad, bad, glad, or disgusted. And, although stories can be looked at as a form of escapism, in the act of storytelling there is more than meets the eye; underlying, subliminal messages are *always* present in these stories.

Through stories you may discover that life itself is a collection of experiences presented in a string of scenes. Put another way, by telling your story, you give others a snapshot of your life and your experiences and, with your stories, you bring together the external, observable, objective world, and your internal conscious and unconscious experiences. In that respect, through the telling of stories you will be able to express who you are. Stories become a way of defining yourself and shaping your sense of self. In your stories, you may talk about your desires, your hopes, and your future plans. They may help understand your place in the world, how you think, and how you make decisions. And via the process of storytelling, you may be trying to solve the riddles that are woven into the stories. Through stories, you are able to create meaning in your life. In essence, stories connect you to a larger self and to universal truths.

The value given to storytelling is demonstrated in the high esteem people often give to the storytellers, those who tell stories. In ancient times there were specialist storytellers whose role it was to keep their audiences updated. These storytellers had many different names, such as minstrel, troubadour, jongleur, trouvère, minnesinger, scald, scop, skaziteli, seanachie, pinkerd, and griot, to name only a few. In our day and age, due to their talents in storytelling, authors, actors, and film directors have become some of the most famous people in the world.

Now that you realize the importance of storytelling, how much attention have you given to telling your own story? By this, I mean, have you ever presented a coherent narrative about the way your life has unfolded? Or, to be more specific, have you ever tried to be the scriptwriter, the producer, and director of your life's documentary? Quite a challenging proposition, isn't it? Of course, you need to decide—depending on what you expect from your audience—what scenes to include or to leave out. In certain aspects, this process is similar to lying on the couch of a psychoanalyst who has asked you to "tell me everything." Realistically, you know that telling everything isn't actually an option. It isn't something you're prepared to do or even can do. You cannot help but try to filter some of the information. However, depending on your courage and willingness to be vulnerable, you may open up somewhat. Whatever you decide to do, however, the request to disclose *everything* will always be a challenging proposition.

If you're prepared to tell your story, however, you should pay attention to how this activity may affect you. What feelings will emerge when you tell your story? What feelings will you have afterwards? To be completely honest about yourself isn't easy and to be asked to "open up" may trigger many defensive reactions. You may have shameful self-beliefs that are very daunting to share. Yet, you may also have a strong desire to share issues that you keep bottled up inside. And to keep bottling them up can be quite stressful. Actually, the need to keep secrets can often be at war with your desire for disclosure.

All things considered, when deciding what story to tell, you need to realize that trying to keep secrets will come with a price. Frequently, what's so harmful about a secret is not the secret itself but rather the mind's compulsion to go over it again and again. In other words, the real harm of secrets is not only that you have the need to hide them, but that you also have to live with them. It is no wonder that, depending on their sensitivity, holding on to your secrets can cause so much emotional discomfort. In fact, the effort required to keep secrets has even been associated with a decrease in physical and psychological well-being.[1]

Concerning secrets, keep in mind that you are not alone in having them. *Everyone has secrets.* Everybody has scars that they prefer to hide. But you can tame the psychological load of secrets with company. Sharing your secrets with people you trust may turn out to be quite comforting. Self-disclosure may lessen rumination and worry. After all, a focused attention on your distress—i.e., obsessing on its causes and consequences as opposed to its solutions—can be detrimental to your mental health. It can prolong or intensify depressive feelings as well as impair your ability to think and process emotions. In contrast, talking about what you perceive to be a secret may become a relief. In fact, self-disclosure through storytelling can contribute to emotional cleansing. It can be a great way to arrive at some form of catharsis and its emotional release can also be an important therapeutic tool for coping with fear, depression, and anxiety.

However, you need to understand that this catharsis can go both ways. You may notice while you're telling your story that a similar cleansing process is taking place for your audience, and you will come to realize that your story can have a great emotional impact on others. As mentioned earlier, storytelling is a great way to build interpersonal connections and stories are the building blocks of empathy and compassion. If you are unwilling to tell your story, it is more than likely that you will remain lonely and isolated. That is why storytelling is so important.

Your personal story can be considered a light that you turn on for yourself.

As may have become clear, telling stories is a way of getting to the heart of who you are. Stories serve some of your most basic needs: passing along your history, dealing with your successes and failings, healing your wounds, engendering hope, and strengthening your sense of community. In more than one way, your personal story can be considered a light that you turn on for yourself: consequently, it will contribute to greater self-awareness and self-knowledge. In that respect, storytelling can be especially powerful if you're prepared to explore different facets of your life: the highs and the lows, the defeats and the successes, the hopes for the future, and even (if you're ready to do so) to bring to the surface your deepest fears. Indeed, exploring your shadow side can help release negative self-beliefs, perhaps giving you an opportunity to re-frame what is troubling you and helping you to accept and integrate these parts of yourself. Thus, stories can be used to empower and humanize, nurturing healing. They can make you more authentic.

Of course, stories have been around since the dawn of time as a means of entertainment, education, cultural preservation, and a way of instilling moral values. As storytelling creatures, narrative imagining—through the communication of stories—has always been a fundamental way of transmitting our thoughts. In fact, the most powerful words in any language are, "Tell me a story." And as is the case with all human beings, your story needs to be told.

If you think about it, many of us, like Molière's M. Jourdain, are already practicing storytelling without realizing it. Reflect on how many times a day you use stories to communicate data, insights, memories, or give commonsense advice. You tell stories to your children, to friends, to people at work, and even to complete strangers who come your way. In addition, subconsciously, you may even be telling stories about yourself inside your head. And in many instances, while you're doing so, you are the hero or heroine in your own story.

THE HERO'S JOURNEY

The psychoanalyst Carl Jung paid much attention to major life dilemmas, suggesting that humans share a collective unconscious repertoire—a set of universal mental themes that influence the way we interact with the world. Among the more common universals in people's stories are the coming of age, the circle of life, the loss of innocence, the power of love, the triumph over adversity, the struggle between good and evil, and the search for power, freedom, truth, and justice. In other words, he is referring to the "Hero's Journey"—a ubiquitous theme in myths, legends, and fables.[2]

From its origins in ancient cave paintings, to fairytales, and on to contemporary movies, the structure of the hero's journey tends to be a familiar one. A hero or heroine goes on an adventure, faces trials, tests, and challenges, is victorious, and in the process, experiences a profound transformation. Most often, the hero's journey is a story about various rites of passage, such as transitioning into an adult, discovering your place in the world, and searching for fulfillment. And while the focus is on attaining some form of transformation and self-realization, the universal story also includes how people cope with anxiety, disappointment, success, heartache, tragedy, and despair. As such, stories operate on multiple levels. On the surface, they deliver facts related to a given time and place. But within each story lie many hidden aspects related to fundamental human (your own) nature and human dilemmas. Therefore, in your role as a storyteller, by describing characters, plots, and settings, you set in motion a process whereby aspects of you that have been lingering in your unconscious will come to the fore. And by expanding your consciousness, you may gain more insights into your inner life. You may attain greater self-knowledge and self-awareness. In other words, the hero's journey is not just a mythological story but a structure deeply embedded within the human psyche. It is an effort to come to terms with your existential dilemmas.

Thus, storytelling is not merely a simple recounting of events. Instead, your stories are crafted representations of events that demonstrate how you have been changing as time passes. It contains the question of how you have experienced your hero's journey. Of course, while doing so, time will play a revisionist role: it writes, erases, and rewrites endlessly. In other words, your story will *always* be a work in progress. Or to be more specific, the story you tell changes depending on your experiences during the various stages of your life. Like a kaleidoscope, the stories will shift with ever-changing parts and points of view.

Your stories are crafted representations of events that demonstrate how you have been changing as time passes.

When you tell your story, of course, it is never solely about you. Storytelling is an interactive process. While telling your story, there is also the question of how your audience experiences your story. What effect will your story have on them? How will they interpret your story in the context of their own challenges? And, as you may have discovered as a storyteller, your story will connect to the personal stories of others. In your story, these people will recognize fragments of their own stories. Consequently, your story may delight, enchant, touch, teach, recall, inspire, motivate, and challenge. Your story may tap into their hidden emotions, making your audience feel angry, depressed, or making them laugh or cry.

Because the telling of your personal story easily connects to the stories of other people's lives, such an interface can help you to deal with most people's greatest existential fear: loneliness. If you tell your story, you may feel less lonesome. It may very well be that your listeners will say, "Yes, I feel the same way. I have had the same experience." And hearing such words can be of considerable comfort. In that respect, stories create feelings of community and interdependency. They give you the feeling that you are not alone in whatever challenges you're facing, that there is meaning to life, that there is ultimately order existing behind what may feel out of control. Hence, stories can help you to make some kind of sense out of why you do what you do and why things happen the way they happen.

What's also quite satisfying when you tell your story is perhaps how hungry your listeners seem to be to hear what you have to say. Even though initially they may not consciously be aware of it, listening to your story will provide them with teachable moments. Your story may encourage them to reflect on their own challenges. They may discover why they behave the way they do or why they're dealing with similar questions. Some of your listeners may even be subjected to unexpected "aha" moments of insight. In this way, stories not only entertain listeners but also give them a resource of proven solutions.

As a storyteller, you should always be aware that you will set into motion a stream of conscious and unconscious associations. And these associations will not only impact your own life but also will have an impact on the lives of others. In other words, when you tell a compelling story, it may affect your listeners deeply. Your personal story could help shape and mold the character of the people who are listening to it, contributing to new stories. Also, as you tell your story, the act of storytelling may encourage you to embark on what before may have seemed to be a very challenging course of action. The same observation can be made for your listeners:

your story may motivate them to take the kind of action they had always been very hesitant to undertake. Consequently, your story may create tipping points for change.

The story you are prepared to tell will very much shape your life, your expectations, and your future actions.

Clearly, the story you are prepared to tell will very much shape your life, your expectations, and your future actions. And as long as you share your story, as long as you're prepared to shed some light on your strengths and vulnerabilities, your hopes, and your dreams, you will be able to create a kind of mutual understanding, the lack of which could distance you from others. And you may discover, as you walk through your story, that you find your way—and so will others.

NOTES

[1] Michael Slepian (2019). "Why the Secrets You Keep Are Hurting You." *Scientific American*, 5 February.
[2] Carl G. Jung (1969). *The Archetypes and the Collective Unconscious*. London: Routledge & Kegan Paul; Joseph Campbell (2008). *The Hero with a Thousand Faces*. New York: New World Library.

2

THE STORYTELLING "CURE"

Those who cannot change their mind cannot change anything.
—George Bernard Shaw

I have been bent and broken, but—I hope—into a better shape.
—Charles Dickens

Although the importance of storytelling for general human functioning has been acknowledged, its potential impact on regulating people's physiological and psychological functioning has received very little attention. And yet, there seems to be a link between storytelling and well-being. Storytelling can have potent therapeutic properties. It appears that sharing personal stories of how to cope with adversity may be beneficial for your mental health. And, while storytelling isn't a fool-proof method of easing mental health problems, uplifting stories can have some amazing benefits on cognitive functioning and mood state.[1] Through the telling of stories, you may be able to move past the problematic issues that are holding you back in life. By challenging unhealthy beliefs and widening the way you view the stories of your life, you

DOI: 10.4324/9781003508939-2

will be able to discover alternative stories, contributing to a more positive outlook to life.

PSYCHOPHYSIOLOGICAL OBSERVATIONS

When you tell a story, you are transferring ideas, thoughts, and emotions into the brains of the people who are listening. In fact, the brain of the storyteller and those of the listeners seem to be synchronizing. Due to the emotional appeal of a story, emotional connections are made. And through this synchronization process meaning and purpose will be shared, creating a common ground that will help make sense of thoughts and feelings. These brain activities enable you to step into other people's shoes, allowing you to enter other worlds and to create new ways of looking at things. And, helped by your imagination, you may become a participant in the story. No wonder that stories create genuine emotions that evoke passionate reactions; emotions experienced not only by the storyteller but also by the listeners.

Stories bring people's brains together.

Here, I need to add that, in the human brain, imagined experiences tend to be processed in the same way as real experiences. Thus, the stories you listen to will create genuine emotions, the sense of presence, and behavioral responses. You will feel emotionally connected to the protagonist of the story. While listening to the story, you might step out of your own shoes, get to understand the other person's point of view, and increase your empathy for the "other."

What seems to be happening is that stories have a neurological effect. Through stories, a transforming process will take place. The same regions of the brain will be activated in the storyteller and the listener. Apparently, when you listen to a story, the neurons in your brain will fire in the same patterns as the neurons of the speaker—a process known as "neural coupling."[2] In fact, learning from the work of neuroscientists—in the context of brain activities—it appears that a well-told story will engage your motor, sensory, and frontal cortexes. These networks are nurtured and solidified by feelings of anticipation of the story's resolution, and involve the input of dopamine—a chemical released in the brain that makes you feel good. Through these neurotransmitters, which are set into motion with the help of stories, you have the opportunity to share other people's grief, joy, and hardships. And this is why, as the result of dopamine being released, the facts will be easier to remember when you experience an emotionally charged event or hear a story of the same nature.

Thus, through storytelling, a process is instigated that is best described as "narrative transportation"—a dynamic and complex interaction between language, text, and imagination which creates a state of cognitive and emotional immersion that deeply engages listeners with the world of the person telling the narrative. And, by means of this process of narrative transportation, stories invite both parties (the storytellers and their listeners) to immerse themselves in the portrayed action and lose themselves for the duration of the narrative.

This narrative transportation process and its plausible origins are most probably based on evolutionarily relevant pre-adaptations involving these aforementioned mirror neuron systems, conversational language structures, metaphor processing abilities, and our imagination. Thus, once a story has sustained your attention long enough, you may begin to emotionally resonate with the story's characters. This "transportation effect" may cause you to have intense, parallel emotional experiences. What is more, during storytelling the listeners' brains also show anticipatory responses, meaning that there could even be an anticipatory coupling effect. And the greater this coupling effect, the stronger the connection will be between the various parties.

To simplify, it seems as if stories bring people's brains together. When listening to stories, not only are the language processing parts of your brain activated but so too are the other areas of your brain that would be used if you were actually part of the story yourself. And, remember, to the human brain, imagined experiences tend to be processed in the same way as real experiences.

Due to this transportation effect—when neural coupling occurs—you tend to forget about your surroundings. You become entirely immersed. Depending on the story, your palms may start to sweat, your heart may have a stronger beat, and your facial expression may change—all signs that you are fully engaged. And, as noted before, as the story unfolds, your brain waves will actually start to synchronize with those of the storyteller. The brain activities of the storyteller and of the listeners will begin to mirror each other. Consequently, the listeners will be weaving their own experiences into the story that they're listening to. In fact, the greater your listening comprehension, the more closely your brain wave patterns will mirror those of the storyteller. This neural transportation effect will be the foundation for feelings of empathy; an important evolutionary, psychological dynamic for social creatures like human beings because it allows you to rapidly forecast the intentions of those you come into contact with. Thus, empathy is not just a nice word; it is something physical and biological originating in your brain and body chemistry.

To the human brain, imagined experiences tend to be processed in the same way as real experiences.

Also, when you connect with the characters in a story, your brain releases the hormone oxytocin, which is associated with connectedness and empathy. It creates an emotional attachment to the characters in the story without having the need for any direct physical or personal contact. And when your brain synthesizes oxytocin, you are inclined to behave in a more trustworthy, generous, charitable, and compassionate manner. In that respect, oxytocin is also often referred to as the trust or love hormone as our bodies release it when we are with people we love and trust, when we hug, or even when we shake hands. It is due to these specific neurological processes that *Homo sapiens* are able to rapidly form relationships with other people. And this human ability to quickly form relationships not only enables large-scale cooperation, it also helps you to foresee whether the people you are dealing with are angry or kind, dangerous or safe, friend or foe. By hearing other people's stories—where they came from, what they do, and who you might know in common—you are able to form relationships. In other words, through storytelling you can create deep emotional connections. However, it needs to be added that certain narratives may also contribute to the release of the stress hormone cortisol in the listeners. Consequently, your understanding of a person's story can become more nuanced. You will experience both positive and negative emotions and, as a result, you may be able to learn about fear, heroism, love, hate, compassion, sorrow, grief, and joy, all from one story, making for a sweet and sour experience. One could say that all change is not growth, as all movement is not moving forward.

STORYTELLING FOR MENTAL HEALTH

What I am pointing out is that apart from the many ways that stories can entertain, inform, influence, and educate, storytelling can also have a curative effect. Storytelling can play a critical role in the maintenance of your mental health. There seems to be a link between narrative and well-being. For example, just as telling other people your life story can have a cathartic effect, storytelling can also be a way to help you reduce your level of stress and anxiety. In fact, your ability to tell stories can have amazing benefits on cognitive functioning and mood state. Thus, telling and listening to stories can be immensely beneficial for improving the quality of your life.

Given the empathic reactions that occur while listening to stories, anyone suffering from mental health issues will be able to connect with others more meaningfully through storytelling. When a person tells his or her story, those who are listening will be inclined to reach out to help when the content of the story warrants action. In other words, storytelling may help people with mental health issues find ways of changing their life situation. The listeners, on hearing a person's story, may be able to suggest alternative ways of dealing with his or her challenges. By taking a different approach to unhealthy beliefs, they may provide a way to transform the course of a person's life. Often, they may be able to provide people who suffer from mental health issues with the kinds of insights that will help them to move forward positively. Thus, storytelling can be a powerful tool for people to gain greater agency.

Therefore, given what we know about storytelling, the question becomes: What psychological dynamics are at work that make storytelling so effective? And how can you use storytelling for better mental health?

- *You are not alone: acknowledging that you have a problem.* Storytelling, as I've already mentioned, provides you with an emotional connection. Telling your story and listening to the stories of others offers a reminder that you are not alone. First, we tend to love stories of people overcoming great adversity. Indeed, many of the oldest stories in existence are about mythical heroes who go on long journeys and conquer myriad obstacles. Second, your story may have similarities with the stories of others. Therefore, while listening to other people's stories, you may come to realize that these people have been down a similar path to you and by sharing what you have gone through could help you to normalize what seemed to you like a bizarre life experience. Somehow, talking about these strange experiences can help you to get them out of your system. Helped by the empathy reflex, you're now connecting to others. Third, by listening to the stories told by others, you obtain insight into the challenges these other people have faced and may or may not have surmounted. This insight can help you to acknowledge that you have a problem—a first step in the process of change. And awareness may be followed by acceptance. In fact, change will never happen if you lack the ability and courage to see yourself for who you are.

  Subsequently, this acceptance might contribute to a desire to find ways to overcome your own challenges. And to some degree this is how support groups like Alcoholics Anonymous and Narcotics Anonymous have used the power of storytelling to their advantage. Also, people suffering from social anxiety, depression, domestic abuse, cancer, and many other conditions have been helped through the process of storytelling.[3]

- *Building self-confidence.* Telling and listening to stories can also build your self-confidence. Hearing the story from someone who has "walked in your shoes" can have a powerful effect. How this other person dealt with the problem might show you the effectiveness of getting help and support. It can help you overcome your feelings of discomfort, fear, shame, or embarrassment about your own experiences. In fact, the very simple act of communing and connecting with other people who have been in the same position can create a profound shift in how you see yourself, possibly helping you overcome your reluctance to acknowledge a troublesome condition or disorder publicly or even to yourself. For many people, the simple realization that they are not alone can make a big difference to how they manage their mental health.

- *Self-observation.* At its core, storytelling is an act of self-discovery. By telling their story in their own way, both the tellers and the listeners can get to the root causes of a condition. The listeners, stimulated by the stories, may begin asking questions—and give their own reflections. By doing so, they give the storytellers a special insight about themselves. In other words, stories beget stories. When you reflect on other people's stories, you create the space to think about your own story. Having a different way of looking at what you are up against can be of help and stories can enable you to understand what contributes to your challenges more clearly. In other words, storytelling can become a powerful vehicle to transfer your life issues to other people, assisting you in the act of sense making.

At its core, storytelling is an act of self-discovery.

In addition, if you want to tell your story, the mere exercise of putting it together will be an act of self-observation and self-analysis. What are you going to include in the story—and what are you going to exclude? What would you like to get help with? Designing the way you will tell your story can help to create distance between the problems you have to deal with and yourself. It gives you a greater perspective on your issues. This process of self-observation will clarify your thoughts. In that respect, storytelling is also a form of externalization. Externalizing the problem, rather than personalizing it, may help you to gain a better focus on how to change unwanted behaviors. It will help you gain greater insight about yourself and could make you feel less self-critical; an attitude that may benefit your sense of self-esteem. Additionally, it could make you more forward-looking, more motivated, and more inclined to make concrete changes to your life.

- *The art of reframing.* By challenging your negative narrative, by bringing some distance to salient experiences, you're taking the first step in reframing unhelpful habitual patterns. You are moving toward a more positive outlook on life. Clearly, an important part of this reframing exercise concerns the ability to emphasize your strengths, which will enable you to come up with an alternative story about the challenges you are facing and achieve the goal of greater self-empowerment. In fact, when you believe that you have more control over your life, your personal story will be seen in a more positive light; that is, as the storyteller, you are recasting the story you're telling about yourself in such a way that it gives your life greater meaning. You are developing a new narrative that honors your past while enabling you to move forward in a much more constructive manner. Taking these actions will enable you to create distance from the difficulties that you're facing. Subsequently, taking a new outlook on life—encouraged by your listeners—you will feel more empowered to make the needed changes in your thought patterns and behavior. You will be able to "rewrite" your life story for the future, reflecting what you're really capable of. However, while doing so, you also need to be aware that personal growth and comfort do not necessarily coexist.

Designing the way you will tell your story can help to create distance between the problems you have to deal with and yourself.

If, however, you are in the listener's role, your challenge will be to deconstruct the stories told by other people—to make them aware of the problematic aspects contained in their stories and how these have been affecting them. Your challenge is to help the storyteller to reframe whatever issues they're facing in a more positive way. You will come to recognize that these people need to rewrite the script of the problematic and dominant storylines and feel able to broaden their view to move toward a healthier outlook on life. This greater awareness will help them smooth out some of the decisions they need to make, to create something that is meaningful and sensible out of the chaos of their lives. And, hopefully, they may come to see how the stories they tell about themselves are affecting their sense of self-esteem—encapsulating how effective they are in dealing with their challenges with people at work and at home. By challenging their unhealthy beliefs and encouraging them to widen the way they view the stories of their life, you're helping these people to find alternative stories that may lead to new and healthier viewpoints for moving forward. In fact, a narrative of transformation can be a powerful part of creating a new future. By reframing their experiences, people may learn how to acquire coping, survival, and resilience skills—and how they can use such skills in the future.

Of course, this exercise isn't just about them, the storyteller, but also about you, the listener. By helping them, you're also helping yourself. Even though you're helping these people to come to terms with the events in their own lives that have left them fearful about the future, self-centered as humans tend to be, it will also have an important effect on you.

- *Inspiring behavior change.* As has become clear by now, storytelling helps to produce behavior change. When you tell your story, you open yourself up to possible new insights or understanding—which can lead to positive change in your life. In other words, a well-told story, given the reactions of the listeners, can be a great vehicle for change. It can mobilize your mind's healing powers. Hearing other people recounting stories of their hurdles and challenges could give you the strength to overcome your own challenges and enable you to face your own fears. In that respect, stories can inspire, motivate, and create action.

Any strongly held view can be influenced by telling a story. Often, if you want to improve the dysfunctional behavior patterns of others, you will be able to model this improvement through a story. By telling these people a story, you can be instrumental in encouraging more functional behavior even if this requires them to change long-held beliefs. After all, the tales you tell hold power-ful sway over memories, behaviors, and even identities.

When you realize that you aren't alone with the challenges that you're facing, when you're prepared to embark on a process of self-observation, when you're ready to reframe the issues that you have to deal with, your task will also be to take a hard look at the stories you're telling yourself. The moment has now come to examine how your personal history and stories are contribut-ing to your present-day problems. The challenge is to attempt to redesign a new narrative that honors your past while enabling you to move forward toward a more constructive future. You need to deconstruct your present narrative to gain greater clarity about your story. Just as fish may not realize they're swimming in water, you may have become so embedded in your own story that you don't know how to get out of it. But having told your story, and having listened to people's reactions, you may be able to unravel the web that you have created for yourself. You may start to become less confused about your story and, with the help of the listeners, able to break down your story into smaller parts, clarifying the problem and making it more solvable.

Just as fish may not realize they're swimming in water, you may have become so embedded in your own story that you don't know how to get out of it.

Deconstruction also involves breaking down the language of a problem, event, or experience to find other possible mean-ings and understandings. In fact, change the way you look at things, and the things you look at may change. Furthermore, in the context of language, deconstruction also involves repur-posing statements to frame your feelings and reactions, rather than externalizing problems by blaming others. Hence, your challenge will be to reframe the problems that you're facing in such a way as to acquire a sense of agency.

Change the way you look at things, and the things you look at may change.

While the starting point of this deconstruction process is the telling of your own story, you need to explore how your problem has served a purpose. You may come to realize that at this point in your life the original purpose of the story has become outdated. Therefore, in the present time, you may want to rewrite the script of your life. You may want to shift the focus of your problem onto your present strengths and resilience, reframing whatever traumatic experiences you may have had in the past. Thus, in rewriting the script of your life, you may need to include how you envision yourself as a person who can cope instead of a person who is fixated on a specific problem. You need to break the cycle of trauma that may have been imposed on you during childhood. You need to recognize your ability to make decisions for yourself and develop your own voice. In fact, by rewriting your story, you're taking back the control that had been held by your problems and survival mechanisms. It will, however, take a good story to help dislodge an unhelpful one. Yet, the right story, told under the right conditions, can have the power to reframe events in an emotionally more positive light, in a way that no number of rational facts could.

By rewriting your story, you're taking back the control that had been held by your problems and survival mechanisms.

- *Creating hope.* What will be important in the art of storytelling is to create for yourself hope for a better future. Instead of leading a life that revolves around your problems, you must construct a more positive identity. Through self-management techniques—which at times may mean asking for professional help—you need to be able to continue to deal with your challenges. Yet, you must be aware that there is always the danger of regression.

In creating this sense of hope, storytelling will be at the heart of your journey of personal growth. Storytelling will help you to normalize the mental health problems that you may be facing. By continuing to share your experiences with other people, not only will you stabilize your own situation but you will also give hope to others and inspire them to face the kinds of challenges that you have dealt with. Your story may actually show the kind of transformation some of the listeners to your story need to go through. Again, through your story, the people listening to you will put themselves in your situation. Doing so helps them see why the choices you made were the right ones. By these means, by showing how you were able to control the *story* of your life, these people, by extension, will be able to control their own lives. In effect, what you should always keep in mind is that you tend to live your life by the stories you tell yourself and others.

What will be important in the art of storytelling is to create for yourself a hope for a better future.

• *Attaining wisdom.* When all is said and done, through storytelling you can gain a more constructive outlook on life. Telling stories of struggle that turn out well may give you the hope you can live a productive life. Such stories could help you to grow wiser in the aftermath of major life challenges. Also, if you're able to tell yourself stories that are hopeful about the future, the confidence that comes from believing in these stories will enable you to persist long enough to develop the competences that are required to achieve whatever goals you have set for yourself. And, as I suggested before, through the telling of your story, you may understand yourself better and find your commonality with others. This resonance will be an aid in meaning-making. Through story listening, you will also gain new perspectives and a better understanding of the world around you. And, via this process, you will challenge and expand your own understanding by exploring how others see and understand the world through their own lens. It will help you understand how and why your life changes.

You tend to live your life by the stories you tell yourself and others.

However, these changes will never happen unless you are prepared to step out of your comfort zone. It is in this "twilight zone" where change begins. And while you are there, keep in mind that all things are difficult before they become easy!

NOTES

[1] Carol Haigh and Pip Hardy (2011). "Tell Me A Story—A Conceptual Exploration of Storytelling in Healthcare Education." *Nurse Education Today*, 31: 408–411; Raymond Berger (2007). "Therapeutic Storytelling Revisited." *American Journal of Psychotherapy*, 61(2): 149–162.

[2] Patrick Colm Hogan (2003). *The Mind and Its Stories: Narrative Universals and Human Emotion*. Cambridge: Cambridge University Press; Jeremy Hsu (2008). "The Secrets of Storytelling: Why We Love a Good Yarn." *Scientific American*, 19(4): 46–51.

[3] Peter Muntig (2016). "Storytelling, Depression and Psychotherapy," in *The Palgrave Handbook of Adult Mental Health*, edited by Michelle O'Reilly and Jessica Lester (pp. 577–596). London: Palgrave Macmillan.

3

THE SCHEHERAZADE METHOD

One of the most popular superstitions consists in the belief that every man is endowed with definite qualities—that some men are kind, some wicked; some wise, some foolish; some energetic, some apathetic, etc. This is not true. We may say of a man that he is oftener kind than wicked; oftener wise than foolish; oftener energetic than apathetic, and vice versa. But it would not be true to say of one man that he is always kind or wise, and of another that he is always wicked or foolish. And yet we thus divide people. This is erroneous. Men are like rivers—the water in all of them, and at every point, is the same, but every one of them is now narrow, now swift, now wide, now calm, now clear, now cold, now muddy, now warm. So it is with men. Every man bears within him the germs of all human qualities, sometimes manifesting one quality, sometimes another; and often does not resemble himself at all, manifesting no change.

—*Leo Tolstoy*

In this chapter, after my exposition of the various facets of storytelling, I wish to attend to the tale of tales—the story of Scheherazade. Of course, you must have heard of Shahrázád, alias Scheherazade, the wife of Shahryār, the Persian king of all kings, known for his hatred of women. This hatred was born out of a love betrayal by his first wife. After discovering her unfaithfulness, he

DOI: 10.4324/9781003508939-3

beheaded her. Subsequently, loathing all womankind, he decided to wed a new woman each day and the next morning put to death his new bride. Yet, as King Shahryār continued his rage-filled revenge, dark clouds gathered over the kingdom. Where there was once gaiety and grace, there was now terror and misery. Clearly, it had become extremely dangerous to be a young woman in the kingdom. To safeguard their daughters, families sought refuge elsewhere.

After several years, all the marriageable women in Shahryār's domain had either been killed or had fled. The only remaining women suitable as brides were Scheherazade and Dinarzade, both daughters to the king's vizier. Given the kingdom's state of distress, the elder, Scheherazade, decided to devise a scheme to save herself and future women from the king's rage. Opposing her father's wishes, she insisted that she enter into marriage with the king. The vizier protested, but eventually gave her his blessing.

On the night of their wedding ceremony, Scheherazade, as her last wish, begged the king for her sister's company, who beforehand she had instructed to ask for a story. After receiving the king's approval to do so, Dinarzade was allowed to visit and, on her sister's request, Scheherazade began to tell her very first tale.

Before dawn, however, she intentionally ended the tale with a cliffhanger, keeping the king in suspense. And, to fan the king's sense of anticipation, she told him that she regretted not finishing her story, and that her next story would have been even more exciting. As the king had become so engrossed in Scheherazade's tale, he permitted her to live another night so that she could finish her tale. But the next evening, Scheherazade would finish the story and begin another, again without concluding it. This she did for one thousand and one nights.

For Scheherazade, the art of storytelling was a matter of life and death. Every day, she played a delicate balancing act of keeping King Shahryār hooked on the story without offending him. But as time passed, and with each tale, King Shahryār began to fall for her beauty, charm, intelligence, and wisdom. Eventually, he realized the injustices he had wrought, and professing his true love for Scheherazade, his vengeful rampage ceased. The kingdom was restored to the great place it once had been. Scheherazade had freed the country of fear. In fact, Shahrázád, in Persian, means "city freer."

Because of her stories, Scheherazade would enter the history books as the narrator of the tales of *One Thousand and One Nights*. According to Western scholars, this collection of tales is really a composite work of popular stories originally transmitted orally and developed over the centuries with material added over time from different places. But whatever the origins of these stories, Scheherazade had drawn from their richness and brought the whole world into the king's bedroom.

Beyond all the tales she told, there was the larger story of Scheherazade and King Shahryār. In that respect, Scheherazade can be considered as one of the shrewdest heroines in world literature. Unwittingly, and without force, King Shahryār was transformed by her simple, yet daring, feminine ruses. By arousing the king's curiosity, and through the morals contained in her stories, she managed to change his outlook on life. From another angle, she could also be considered a highly effective psychotherapist, life coach, or general change agent; a person experimenting with an innovative method of psychological intervention. Thus, although she voluntarily married a mass murderer, through her stories, she guided him into becoming a moral, loving husband.

PSYCHOLOGICAL JUDO

The king's transformation occurred because Scheherazade knew how to harness the power of stories. As I mentioned in the Introduction to this book, storytelling itself has always been a bedrock of the human experience, going back to the dawn of time. Scheherazade, however, very subtly used psychological processes as she was telling her stories to the king.[1] To begin with, she was astute enough not to confront King Shahryār directly with his evil deeds. Instead, she would harness the power of *psychological judo*—which is to move with, and not against, whatever needs to be dealt with—so as to break down the other person's defenses and influence the outcome.

Scheherazade would harness the power of psychological judo—which is to move with, and not against, whatever needs to be dealt with.

Judo is a Japanese martial art form meaning "gentle way." In judo, if someone throws a punch, the momentum is used in a way the opponent does not expect, causing them, momentarily, to be off balance. And it is in this moment of off balance that the judoka will have the chance to influence the next move and to score a point. Likewise, psychological judo can be a highly effective way to influence your opponent gently, whether this means to share his or her own opinion, help the person in question to see another perspective, or by encouraging him or her to find a different path.

As a highly effective psychological judoka, Scheherazade realized that King Shahryār had deep and powerful emotionally based defenses around his beliefs (that his acts of vengeance were justified given the behavior of his disloyal wife). To confront these beliefs head on would only have reinforced them, making it much harder for him to be open to change. Instead (as in judo), Scheherazade rolled with his resistances. She approached him without being judgmental about his actions, at least not overtly. Adopting a nonconfrontational approach, she showered King Shahryār with a thousand different stories, drawing from the wisdom of the ages, and by so doing slowly redirected his hostile energy to take on different perspectives. At the same time, she broke down his defenses through showing genuine compassion and demonstrating that she understood why he was acting in this particular manner.

Scheherazade's story is still relevant today, as we continue to see women battling for survival in a highly paternalistic world. Women still have to fight to make their own choices, to live according to their beliefs about freedom, sexuality, and love. Thus, Scheherazade's way of dealing with the king can be seen as a method for how to influence people and get them to change.

THE STORYTELLING CURE

Through her stories, Scheherazade taught the king about the ways of women, exposing him to basic emotions like happiness, sadness, fear, disgust, anger, contempt, surprise, shame, and guilt, and finally toward forgiveness. She guided him to these revelations cleverly, camouflaging the central theme of forgiveness within a succession of stories.

Through the morality of each tale, she illustrated the disastrous outcome for characters who behaved in a cruel manner similar to himself. At the same time, step by little step, she sympathized with him and the betrayal he suffered, but also made him see the link between immediate gratification (finding satisfaction in acting out his rage toward women) and the longer-term adverse consequences (the devastating effects on his kingdom). In doing so, she introduced doubt into the king's mind concerning the value of his motivations and his actions, creating an opening for change.

To further facilitate the transformation process, she emphasized self-efficacy and helped to increase the king's confidence in his ability to change. Applying her intervention technique of psychological judo, she did not tell him directly what to do but instead guided him to self-awareness and self-knowledge—to know what he did and also what he was all about—and to take responsibility for his actions and the ownership of finding a solution.

Clearly, Scheherazade succeeded in transforming King Shahryār. Using storytelling as a way to connect and to challenge, she altered his outlook on life and humanized him. Although she entered the king's chambers as a prisoner, as time went by, it was he who became enslaved by her charm, intelligence, and character.

To summarize, here are a number of steps that can be taken by anyone interested in creating change in people using the Scheherazade intervention method:

- Be an astute observer of the behavior of the person you're dealing with and create the link between action and consequence.
- Create doubt in this person's mind about the value of his or her present behavior.
- Deal with this person in a subtle, seemingly inconspicuous manner, and avoid being argumentative.
- Do not impose your point of view and resist the temptation to directly tell the person the path that he or she needs to take. Direct advice might cause the person to back off or to resist.

- Carefully listen to what the person has to say and show a great deal of empathy with the issues he or she is preoccupied with.
- Work to better understand the source of a person's worries and insecurities and help him or her disentangle ambivalent feelings about his or her behavior to find the required trajectory for behavior change.
- Empower the person to explore his or her own ideas and identify more appropriate ways of living and alternative behaviors. Support him or her in creating multiple plans of action.
- In a very respectful manner, help the person weigh the various alternatives and honor his or her ability to manage these changes themselves.

While Scheherazade's tale was set in the Islamic Golden Age, between the eighth and fourteenth centuries, in present times many of you will still find yourself in difficult life situations that require change. But, as you may also have discovered, changing behavior can be extremely difficult. Fortunately, the Scheherazade storytelling approach is a form of psychological intervention that can be applied in many different situations that require change both in an individual's personal and professional life. Through the use of subtle storytelling, you can help people identify the roadblocks and obstacles that stop them from living a fulfilling life. By using psychological judo—moving with rather than against resistances—you can encourage them to explore their views and perspectives on things and, more deeply, their values, priorities, interests, feelings, moods, wishes, dreams, fears, and apprehensions. In a nonthreatening way, you can help them to confront and overcome their anxieties and insecurities and stop dysfunctional behavior patterns. And, if done well, possible lifestyle changes may become open for discussion.

Through the use of subtle storytelling, you can help people identify the roadblocks and obstacles that stop them from living a fulfilling life.

In fact, the Scheherazade intervention technique shows once again how words and storytelling can change our world. After all, if you're able to change the mindset of a mass murderer, you should be able to change anybody!

NOTE

[1] To understand this psychological methodology, see also William R. Miller and Stephen Rollnick (2023). *Motivational Interviewing: Helping People Change and Grow*. New York: Guilford.

4

LEADERS WHO TELL STORIES RULE THE WORLD

If you would win a man to your cause, first convince him that you are his sincere friend. Therein is a drop of honey that catches his heart, which, say what he will, is the great high road to his reason.

—Abraham Lincoln

He turned those dry bones of history and dirty records of misdeeds into things to weep or to laugh over.

—Rudyard Kipling

The Mole was bewitched, entranced, fascinated. By the side of the river he trotted as one trots, when very small, by the side of a man who holds one spellbound by exciting stories; and when tired at last, he sat on the bank, while the river still chattered on to him, a babbling procession of the best stories in the world, sent from the heart of the earth to be told at last to the insatiable sea.

—Kenneth Grahame

"Do we have to go through this again?" Lucas¹ mumbled silently to himself. "This is information overload. One PowerPoint slide packed with information after the other. Does our CEO really expect us to

DOI: 10.4324/9781003508939-4

digest all this information? Doesn't he realize that he is overdoing it? And look at the others in the room, the energy seems to be drained from them too. Most of them are not listening or paying attention. Some aren't even subtle about it; they have closed their eyes. The way our CEO is making presentations—the convoluted means by which he is presenting the story of the company—is such a waste of time!"

Does this scene sound familiar to you? Meetings with too much information that leave you feeling utterly exhausted? And, you wonder, why does it have to be this way? Are there not better ways to engage the audience and get people's attention?

As I have emphasized before, storytelling is a powerful way to communicate and connect to people. There is much truth to the statement: tell me a fact, and I may forget, but tell me a story, and it will stay in my mind for ever. Purposeful storytelling isn't showbusiness; it's excellent business. And yet, unfortunately, it is an underrated skill among many executives.

Tell me a fact, and I may forget, but tell me a story,
and it will stay in my mind for ever.

The dialogue created through stories provides the context, meaning, and opportunity to enable relationships. Through stories, people can help one another to see and feel what they themselves see and feel. The emotional associations evoked through stories can also be magical, transporting listeners into the story themselves. Through this experience, the listeners receive information that could lead them to attain greater insights about their own lives. Yet, despite the great value of storytelling, it has remained a form of exchange that is often overlooked.

If we turn back to the vignette, we can see that the inability of Lucas's CEO to tell a good story undermined his ability to be an engaging leader. Effective leaders know how to tell a good story. And they know that, in doing so, they will be able to take their people on an emotional journey, sketch their vision for their organization's future, and subsequently align their people behind this vision.

Both in politics and in business, leaders who are great storytellers are also the ones who have been able to accomplish great deeds. As an example, Nelson Mandela was a master storyteller. He always used his personal experiences when he tried to solve seemingly intractable social problems. With the help of stories, he went to great lengths trying to transform South Africa into a rainbow nation. Also, the power of storytelling was very much utilized by the late Steve Jobs of Apple. To use his own words: "The most powerful person in the world is the storyteller. The storyteller sets the vision, values, and agenda."[2] And as a storyteller, he introduced game-changing products such as iTunes, iPhones, and the iPad.

Thus, even though storytelling may be seen as a simple dialogue between the narrator and the listener, great storytellers such as Mandela and Jobs are able to ignite the imaginations of their listeners. In contrast to Lucas's CEO, they realized that whereas facts and numbers would alienate people, great stories would have the power to draw people in. Again, it is stories that inspire, motivate, and challenge us.

Therefore, it is not far-fetched to say that leaders who are talented storytellers rule the world. They recognize that stories can be the most powerful instrument in their communication toolbox. They know that if they are able to tell a story well, people will remember the core message even if they don't remember all of the details. Clearly, storytelling is the mother of all communication techniques. Great stories linger on. Great stories will help the listeners remember ideas and concepts in a way that a convoluted, number-prone PowerPoint presentation will never do. In fact, telling stories is the best way to bake information into a person's brain. Thus, people in a leadership position who fail to grasp or use the power of stories risk failure in whatever they're trying to accomplish. As I pointed out before, stories create shared emotions, foster presence, and encourage empathic behavioral responses. Emotional connection also sets in motion associative thinking, where listeners link the themes in the story to their own life stories.

Effective leaders know how to tell a good story.

Due to the neurological processes that are ignited through storytelling, the emotional repertoire of both the storyteller and his or her listeners goes into overdrive. Here, what should be kept in mind is that the purpose of emotions is to alert us to challenging situations. In that respect, emotions function very much like a thermostat, providing warning signals to the people who are listening to the storyteller. They indicate that they should pay attention. They also explain why a process of associative thinking will be set in motion if a story is captivating, creating the kind of imagery that is related to the question of how the listeners should go about solving their own life dilemmas. That's the reason why compelling stories have such a strong impact. Essentially, if storytellers are able to touch their listeners emotionally by having them associate with various life themes, the listeners will foster strong identification with the challenges faced by the storyteller.

All of us, as reflected in our story, struggle to come to terms with the meaning and purpose of our life, how we can cope with the inescapably difficult and puzzling facts of our existence, and how the many seemingly insurmountable hindrances can be overcome along the way. Yet, many of these stories also contain an element of hope and, if we take the right steps, there can be light at the end of the tunnel. At one of the crossroads in this journey, there may be an epiphany—a moment of awareness or realization of how to transcend the challenges that need to be dealt with. And if this happens, it is as if a lightbulb switches on in the hero's or heroine's mind. This is their "aha!" or "eureka!" moment, that specific point in their journey when they have found a way to resolve their predicament. The story has created a *tipping point for change*.

It is stories that delight, enchant, touch, teach,
inspire, motivate, and challenge.

Leaders who use the storytelling approach will be highly effective if they access major human concerns within their stories. By referring in their narratives to these universal themes, they connect to their listeners' longings, fears, and frustrations, affecting their audience emotionally. Essentially, they transport their audience from their humdrum existence to a world of inquiry, exploration, and quests. They will transport them to a world beyond, helping them to cross boundaries of time, space, and imagination. Leaders with a deep understanding of the psychological processes within storytelling will utilize narrative as the secret weapon in their arsenal to create the emotional glue that connects them to their audience, helping them to cement ideas in a way that the presentation of facts and data will never do. And by presenting their narrative in a compelling way, they can move their audience from apathy, to empathy, toward action.

NOTES

[1] All characters portrayed in the case studies are fictional.

[2] Anecdote on meeting Steve Jobs by Tommy Blackrose when he worked at NeXT in 1994. Published on Quora. https://www.quora.com/What-are-the-best-stories-about-people-randomly-or-non-randomly-meeting-Steve-Jobs

5

STORIES THAT PLEAD FOR HELP

Explore, and explore, and explore. Be neither chided nor flattered out of your position of perpetual inquiry. Neither dogmatise yourself, nor accept another's dogmatism.

—Ralph Waldo Emerson

Wie sollten wir jener alten Mythen vergessen können, die am Anfange aller Völker stehen; der Mythen von den Drachen, die sich im äußersten Augenblick in Prinzessinnen verwandeln; vielleicht sind alle Drachen unseres Lebens Prinzessinnen, die nur darauf warten, uns einmal schön und mutig zu sehen. Vielleicht ist alles Schreckliche im tiefsten Grunde das Hilflose, das von uns Hilfe will. *

—Rainer Maria Rilke

Our prime purpose in this life is to help others. And if you can't help them, at least don't hurt them.

—Dalai Lama

---

* Translation: How can we forget those old myths that stand at the beginning of all peoples; the myths of dragons who transform into princesses at the last moment; Maybe all the dragons in our lives are princesses just waiting to see us beautiful and brave. Maybe, deep down, everything terrible is the helpless thing that wants help from us.

DOI: 10.4324/9781003508939-5

To continue this storytelling track, let me tell you another story. It is the story of Carla, a senior executive at a global chemical firm. Here is what she was experiencing.

Being in a black hole

Carla felt like she had sunk into a deep black hole. As things stood, life seemed to have very little to offer. There was just too much on her plate. To begin with, the pressures at work were really getting to her. Given her company's reliance on energy, she couldn't recall a more turbulent time. Nevertheless, despite the emergency—and despite the fact that her direct reports were quite competent—she had been very reluctant to ask them for help. She believed that they already had enough to do. Still, Carla didn't fully understand what held her back from asking for their assistance. Whatever the reasons were, however, she had always felt that she should be able to manage things on her own.

Apart from the stress at work, there were also pressures in her personal life. As things stood, her home life was quite messy. The children were at a difficult age and needed a lot of attention. Taking care of them took a large amount of her energy. And her husband wasn't much help. To ask him to do something always seemed to be a struggle. In fact, rare were the occasions when she dared to ask him to become more involved in the household. As it was, it was up to her to keep everything in balance. At times, she felt like a circus juggler, trying to keep too many balls in the air.

Of course, Carla realized that this circus act wasn't new to her. She had a long history of keeping too many balls in the air. In fact, her present situation led her down memory lane, to when she was a child. At that time, it had also been up to her to keep things going. Sometimes, reflecting on her childhood experiences, she wondered who had been the adult? Who had been taking care of whom? Far too often, she was placed in the caretaker role. It had always been her responsibility to take care of her depressed mother. And her father hadn't been a lot of help as he wasn't around much. It made her wonder whether it was her role in life to take care of others? This memory led Carla again to the question of why it was so difficult for her to ask other people for help. Why did the very act of asking for support make her feel so uncomfortable?

Listening to Carla's story, it becomes obvious that she shouldn't feel this way. She should remind herself that humans are social creatures. *Homo sapiens* evolved by living in a group setting. In fact, without helping each other, the human species wouldn't be where it is today. To give and receive help has always been one of our defining characteristics. Still, despite this all too human quality, some people (Carla being a good example) seem to be very reluctant to tell their story—and ask others for help, even though they know they can't accomplish everything on their own. They struggle to reach out when they're in need. Yet, at the same time, these people will go out of their way to help others when asked.

Carla's story raises some questions. Do you find it hard to tell people that you need help? Are you someone who prefers to do everything by yourself? Even when you are at your wits' end, are you, like Clara, still reluctant to reach out to other people—to tell your story of woe? If so, you need to remind yourself that you are not alone. There are many people like you. And, if that is the case, why are you so hesitant to reach out? What is holding you back? What is your story?

PSYCHOLOGICAL BARRIERS THAT PREVENT YOU FROM ASKING FOR HELP

Looking deeper into the inability of some people to ask for help, various psychological processes seem to be at play, which involve the intricacies of attachment behavior, shame, guilt, trust, and pride. Taking a deep dive into these psychological dynamics, specific patterns can be found that explain why people are so reluctant to seek assistance. These patterns aren't necessarily exclusive; people can be subjected to a number of them, and more than one pattern can contribute to a person's reluctance to make demands on other people. Let's list a few.

- *The fear of being vulnerable.* For some people, asking for help is seen as a sign of weakness. Issues centered around self-esteem appear to be at play here. They are greatly concerned about how others perceive them and, consequently, asking for help brings up very negative connotations. It means being seen as weak, being a failure, being incompetent, being inferior, to be seen as a loser. In addition, the very idea of asking for support leaves these people mired in shame. It makes them feel exposed. Furthermore, given their fear of having others see how vulnerable they are, these people may also have intimacy issues—having people getting too close—as asking for help is an invitation for closeness. The whole process makes them nervous and uncomfortable. And, given their feelings of insecurity, the fear is that, by being too close, others may see their real self. They would see their vulnerabilities, discovering the real person behind their carefully constructed façade.

- *The need to be independent.* These people prioritize self-reliance and self-sufficiency. For them, asking for help has negative associations with asking for a handout. Given this particular outlook on life, such people strongly believe that they should be able to do everything by themselves. Quite incorrectly, they think that they should be capable of handling any situation. In fact, the ability to do things on their own is important for their self-image. And perhaps, given their family and cultural background, it is as if they are hardwired for independence. Some of these people may even be counter-dependent, living with the leitmotif of "I don't need anyone, I can do things by myself." No wonder that they prefer to play the role of the lone ranger, pretending to have superpowers that allow them to do it all. However, this go it alone attitude will not be helpful in work situations or in the context of family life where the emphasis should be on teamwork and mutual cooperation.

- *The fear of losing control.* Some people will not ask for help given their concerns of being indebted to another person. Allowing someone else to help will be equated with losing control. Owing anything to another person makes for feelings of dependency and a loss of autonomy, feelings that they find difficult to tolerate. In addition, they are focused on the idea that if they do receive support, they may then have to reciprocate, creating the concern whether they are able to do so (or even want to do so). Thus, part of their uneasiness around losing control is their fear of being indebted to others. It makes them fearful that, by asking someone else for help, the power balance in a relationship will shift. They are afraid that others will make them do their bidding because they have helped them. Consequently, given their sense of pride, such people would rather suffer alone with their problems than ask someone else for a favor. Quite often, however, there are trust issues behind these concerns. People who struggle with trust will find it difficult to entrust their fate to someone else (even if the person has no ill intentions and is willing to help). Again, trusting others may be equated with losing control.

- *The fear of rejection.* Some people are afraid to ask for a favor or anything else from another person because they overestimate the likelihood of rejection. They are afraid of hearing people say "no" to their requests. They fear that whatever they ask, it will be refused. In fact, behind their reluctance to ask for help is a fear of being humiliated, ridiculed, or misunderstood. Some of these people (at least symbolically) equate rejection with annihilation, an attack on their whole being. No wonder that the idea of rejection is so devastating. Unfortunately, they don't realize that there could be many reasons why the person who is being asked for help would not be available. It is very possible that the person who says "no" when asked would be very willing to be helpful in the future and it was just that the timing of the request was off. Of course, in the context of this fear of rejection, there are some who may have been burned in the past. Yet, it is important to realize that this doesn't mean that the same thing will happen again. However, given their previous experiences, rejection is, ultimately, what they expect.

- *The danger of being over-empathic.* Overly empathic people not only sense others' emotions strongly but also take too much responsibility for easing their concerns. They imagine that they can only win love by taking care of others. It's their belief that they should *always* put the needs of others before their own. This may not seem like a bad thing, but it means that, at the same time, they hide and do not take care of their own needs. They are terrible at self-care. In fact, they feel guilty for imposing on others' time, energy, and goodwill, always worrying about being seen as a burden. Basically, they don't want to appear entitled, to be labelled as selfish. Truth be told, they don't believe that they have ever earned the privilege of making a request and it is their strong belief that other people have much better things to do than deal with their problems. Obviously, in the context of their own needs and the needs of others, there seems to be a great cognitive dissonance.

- *A sense of victimization.* Some people never ask for help because they go through life with the mantra "I don't deserve to be helped, I'm not worthy." They have a "poor me" attitude to life. They believe it is their fate to struggle to do things all on their own. Living is equated with self-sacrifice, with martyrdom. It is as if they secretly believe that they are supposed to suffer. And this victim mentality prevents them from asking for help. In that respect, it is as if such people are on a journey of self-sabotage. They seem to be listening constantly to an inner voice telling them that they're not good enough. For them, reaching out will not be an option. Yet, wallowing in self-pity doesn't make their situation any better. They will let any problem they have fester without calling for support.

A LACK OF SELF-KNOWLEDGE

Clearly, many of the psychological barriers listed here involve self-esteem issues. Those suffering from such barriers perceive themselves in a very negative and critical light and seem to be extremely hard on themselves. They believe that they simply aren't good enough to deserve other people's time and energy. It is no wonder that they undervalue and neglect their own needs, putting those of others before their own. They are unable, therefore, to tell their story of woe. In fact, they interpret the need to ask for help as a confirmation of their own inferiority. And given their lack of self-knowledge, they may not even recognize their self-sabotaging behavior. In reality, many of these people don't understand what self-management—how to manage themselves vis-à-vis other people—is all about. In creating a life for themselves that is worth living, they have no clear understanding of what they really need to ask for and do not understand how others can help them. Thus, unless they gain a greater awareness of the things they are struggling with, they simply won't be able to express their needs clearly and will, instead, hang on to a false sense of independence.

Of course, there's nothing wrong with being independent. There's nothing wrong in making decisions on your own. But, at the same time, you should realize that human life is embedded in a web of relationships. As mentioned before, collaboration is an important part of what makes you human. It is what makes society work. However, this also means that you have to reach out when you find it difficult to do things by yourself. You should not expect other people to be mind readers. Instead, you need to make clear that you would appreciate their help. It needs to be stressed, however, that if you show too much of an independent streak, you will make others think that you don't need help even when the time has come when you do.

Collaboration is an important part of what makes you human.

The million-dollar question therefore becomes: Do you want to go through life with the imagery of being a lone wolf? Do you really think that it will make for a fulfilled life? Are you prepared, instead, to accept that there is nothing shameful in asking for help? Have you realized that pretending to be an island unto yourself is not going to be the answer? Perhaps you would be much better off joining the human race? There are going to be times when you need to accept that what's demanded of you is beyond your present capacity. It is exactly at those times when you should be open to the idea of asking for help and, in fact, such times will come for all of us. However, as Carla's example illustrates, your previous life experiences could make asking for this help quite difficult. Clearly, if you are programmed to have to cope by yourself, reaching out will not be easy. Nevertheless, you would be wise to make the effort to get yourself out of this rabbit hole. Obviously, it is high time that Carla has a deeper understanding of her own story and learns how to reframe it. And this comment is relevant for everybody who has difficulties in asking for help.

DECIPHERING ORIGINS

So why are you in this rabbit hole, unable to ask for help? Often this particular rabbit hole has been created by parents who were unable or unwilling to offer unconditional love and support. In many instances, adverse childhood experiences such as neglect and abuse are the cause of a reluctance to ask for help. Abuse, in particular, is a highly effective way to destroy children's sense of self-worth. Abused children may end up with self-limiting beliefs about themselves. They may even imagine that they're "bad," that they deserve to suffer—and that they don't even have the right to ask for help. Thus, as a coping strategy, these children may feel compelled to please others as a form of maintaining contact or, alternatively, they will try to be invisible, to make very few demands. Nevertheless, there is always the option for these people to work with and rewrite these scripts later in life once they understand what has happened to them in their childhood.

REWRITING THE SCRIPT IN THE INNER THEATER

Without a rewrite of their personal story, people such as Carla are complicating their lives. Clearly, human progress has always been about give and take and, thus, a lack of reciprocity in relationships does not move people forward. It begs the question, therefore, of how people who are reluctant to ask for help can be helped? What can be done to encourage them to reach out? Fortunately, people who find themselves in this predicament have a number of options:

- *Make a SMART request.* One option is that these people could learn to make a SMART request. SMART is a well-known acronym for an entreaty that's **S**pecific, **M**easurable, **A**chievable, **R**elevant, and **T**ime-bound. What this means is that when you ask for help, you need to make the request specific (explain why you need help and what needs to be accomplished); measurable (to make sure progress can be tracked); achievable (clarify that it can be done); relevant (don't put up a request for help if it isn't really necessary); and time-bound (set a deadline). Also, while pondering the idea of a SMART request, ask yourself what is it that is holding you back from doing so? Perhaps you don't really know how to go about it? Possibly, you don't even know how to start such a conversation around help. And, what's more, you may not know who to ask. That said, if, however, you can gather the courage to ask for help, you need to think about who has the skills, the ability, or the knowledge to help you effectively. You should also give some thought to the question of who is likely to respond positively to such a request. In that context, it may be helpful to think of people who have offered to help you in the past. Perhaps, at that time, despite their willingness to help, you didn't take them up on the offer? What you should also keep in mind is that the timing of asking for help will be important. When you ask for help, you should give the other party time to consider the request. It also isn't considerate to ask for help when the other party is stressed out or in a bad mood. An effective strategy to encourage the other party to offer help willingly can be to formulate the request as a conversation rather than a transaction. In other words, what makes help more forthcoming is talking through what is needed with the potential helper and perhaps exploring what both of you can do together. Doing it this way not only makes asking for help more respectful but also allows for the development of a deeper connection with the person you are asking for assistance, which may lead to a learning experience for both parties.

- *Reframe, reframe, reframe.* To help you to overcome your reluctance to ask for help, try to reconceptualize your needs by looking at them from a different perspective. If you continue to view asking for help as a weakness, you are likely entering a path to failure. You have to reframe the situation to turn it into a win–win situation for both parties. For example, you would do well to ask yourself: If I don't ask for help, what will the consequences be? By thinking about the worst outcome and how it could affect others—and perhaps the potential for disaster—you should be able to accept the idea that you have a right to ask for assistance, that asking for help isn't necessarily imposing a burden on someone. In fact, looking at it in this way, by asking for help you may actually be helping everybody. Of course, if you take this route, it means that you may also need to tear down your façade of being strong and self-sufficient. Instead, you will need to replace it with the strength of being just an ordinary mortal. And even if your request for help is rejected, which can happen for myriad reasons unrelated to yourself, do not view such a rejection as a catastrophe. Try to figure out why this has happened and look on it as a learning experience. Most often, when people cannot help you, they will give you a reason why or suggest an alternative to your request. It could very well be that the timing of your request was bad or that the person who you have asked doesn't have the resources (or answers or tools) to help you. Thus, an aspect of asking for help is also to understand that it won't always work out exactly as you would like. After all, other people also have deadlines to meet and other constraints on their time. Taking such a reflective position may help you when formulating future requests (it could make you realize that you need to give people a bit more time to plan to help you, or that you should think more about *who* to ask before you reach out) or even encourage you to change a request.

If you continue to view asking for help as a weakness, you are likely entering a path to failure.

- *Communicate, communicate, communicate.* You may have discovered by now that if you find it difficult to ask for help, you will end up being quite alone. You are distancing yourself from other people and, by doing so, you are making it very hard for others to get to know you. Thus, when you find you are under too much pressure, you should make an effort to talk openly about what you are going through and what you would like to get help with. People shouldn't have to guess your needs or wants. If you don't communicate openly yet expect other people to understand your needs and to come to the rescue, the outcome is predictable. Again, it is imperative to remind yourself that the people you are dealing with aren't mind readers. Thus, don't be cryptic. Don't cry for help in silence. And, although you may blame them for leaving you in the lurch, in reality they simply may not be aware of what's happening to you. Therefore, don't just drop hints or wait around hoping for others to offer their assistance. Instead, try to be direct and clearly say what you need help with, and why. Make it easy for the other person to decide if they can offer help or not, and make clear that you need commitment, not charity. Although it's true that you don't have the right to demand assistance, you do have the right to ask. Of course, by deciding to communicate your needs and wants, this also means that you should try to trust others. Try to accept other people's good intentions, and to believe that they'll be open about whether or not they can help you. In addition, make sure to communicate your request in such a way that gives the people you're communicating with a way out. You don't want to make them feel guilty if they say no, no matter what the reasons may be. In other words, when you are asking someone for assistance, make it as easy as possible for them to say no to your request.

Don't cry for help in silence.

- *Practice, practice, practice.* You should practice asking for and receiving help. Although in the beginning it may be uncomfortable for you to ask for help, remind yourself that it is an important life skill. And, as with any skill, asking for help will get easier the more you practice it. As a learning experience of how asking for help makes you feel, try to make an effort to reflect on your emotions when you're doing so. It may be an interesting learning experience. And even when you have adverse emotional reactions, summon your courage and ask anyway. Of course, a good approach is to start asking for help from people you are most comfortable with, perhaps a family member or a coworker you trust. But once you feel more at ease, you should test your new-found skills with someone with whom you are a bit less familiar. And, while practicing, keep on reminding yourself that human beings are hardwired to connect, that we're innately "programmed" to help each other. If someone does agree to help you, it is important to receive his or her help gratefully. Let the helper take ownership of what he or she has agreed to do, even if it means giving up a modicum of control. Furthermore, be sure to thank the person after he or she has helped you out and take a moment to reflect on how you are making him or her feel by doing so.

- *Seek out a coach or psychotherapist.* If, despite all these recommendations of how to go about asking for help, you are still very reluctant to do so, you would do well to heed the old saying that "A problem shared is a problem halved." If you have strong emotional reactions when asking for help, you may benefit from professional mental health support. Often, a coach or psychotherapist will be able to give you more clarity about the matter. They may help you to unravel the blockages that are preventing you from asking for help. They may enable you to tell a different story about yourself. Of course, it may be difficult for you to make the decision to see such a person and, at times, you might need the help of friends or family members to enable you to take such an initiative. After all, it can be very hard for someone who never asks for help to reach out and book a session with a mental health professional. If you do decide to do so, however, you should also remind yourself that you are paying for the experience. You are not just asking for a favor. Hopefully, such a reminder can make the decision to take this initiative feel less threatening. And once you have entered into such a therapeutic or coaching relationship—experiencing what it's like to be supported and championed—you can get a taste for just how good it feels to be helped. From that point onwards, your mental health professional can then work with you to grow your confidence to get your needs met in all areas of your life.

A SUMMING UP

You need to remind yourself that asking for help is not a weakness. In fact, it will be the bravest thing that you can do. Trying to be an island unto yourself isn't the answer. On the contrary, you should look at asking for help as a way to join the human race. It forces you to put your trust in others. And, conversely, it also allows them to trust you. Asking for help does not show you are weak but allows others to relate to you. It strengthens the bonds with those who are helping you. By opening up and telling your story, it shows that you too are an imperfect human being like everyone else. And in doing so, you will discover that by showing your vulnerabilities, you will open the door for others to approach you when they need your assistance, which will create a strong bond. Also, when you share your vulnerabilities and ask for help to overcome them, other people will see you more as a whole person.

Asking for help does not show you are weak but allows others to relate to you.

Your story of help could be reframed as a social adventure: others will learn more about you when you tell your story and you will learn more about those to whom you tell it. You will learn about their strengths and passions. By asking for help, you will get to know them better. Paradoxically, asking for help or advice could make you seem smarter, more confident, and more competent. By learning to ask others for help, both parties can grow and learn like everyone else. Refusing to ask for help when you need it is refusing someone the chance to be helpful.

You should also realize that when you ask someone for a helping hand, it will often make them happy because they're able to give you something. Allowing other people to give makes them feel better. The happiest people are those who do the most for others. Therefore, when others help, they are also helping themselves. When you ask for support, you are thus letting others experience the happiness that comes from giving. You are enabling them to share their gifts and talents. You are allowing them to shine. Consequently, you are not just serving yourself. You are helping others to grow while you grow with them. And by gaining knowledge from those who know more about certain things than you do, it shows that you are willing to learn.

> *Your story of help could be reframed as a social adventure: others will learn more about you when you tell your story and you will learn more about those to whom you tell it.*

Furthermore, when you are able to obtain help, you will have more time to take care of yourself and your own needs. You will have a greater opportunity to do the things that you enjoy, giving you the chance to focus on what matters most to you in life and making you more in harmony with yourself, which will benefit your mental health.

Therefore, don't make the mistake of not asking for help. Be smart enough to know when you need it and always remind yourself that one of the biggest defects in life is the inability to ask for help. In this context, it is useful to think about the story of the turtle. If you see a turtle up on top of a fence post, you know that it didn't get there on its own; it must have had some help. So, take the opportunity to adapt your story. Be brave, by being vulnerable!

6

THE GOLDEN LARVA SYNDROME

No longer talk at all about the kind of man a good man ought to be, but be such.

—Marcus Aurelius

One doesn't discover new lands without consenting to lose sight of the shore, for a very long time.

—André Gide

He who knows others is wise;
He who knows himself is enlightened.

—Lau-Tzse, Tao te Ching

SNATCHING DEFEAT FROM THE JAWS OF VICTORY

Why was Stephen going nowhere? His educational record had been quite promising. He had successfully graduated from a well-known university and then gone on to finish an MBA at a premier business school. With this excellent record, he was rapidly hired by an elite financial services firm.

After taking up this position, Stephen was initially successful, but this promising start did not last long. A number of ill-judged

DOI: 10.4324/9781003508939-6

decisions later, his supervisors no longer trusted his competence and his career stalled; essentially, he became "baggage" to the organization. Stephen decided to move on, changing companies to start afresh. Unfortunately, the same pattern occurred again—after a great start, it was not long before he went off the rails. Stephen seemed to be a master of self-defeatism.

So, what is it that holds Stephen back from achieving his full potential? Why does he seem to resort repeatedly to acts of self-sabotage? What is the story within his story?

There are no easy answers to these questions, only that there are various psychological dynamics at work. In the context of Stephen's career, it is fair to say he exhibits some classic "golden larva" behaviors. On paper and initial performance, he is an individual who appears extremely promising, but ends up stalling, or worse, sabotaging that initial success entirely. Like caterpillars, talented people like Stephen are expected to grow and make something out of their lives, yet they get stuck at the larval stage, never develop into butterflies, and never spread their wings.

History books are littered with gifted young people like Stephen who, as adults, fail to continue their path to bigger and better things. Conversely, there are adults who are less than remarkable children but who, later, create incredible careers. The question is, what are the differentiating factors? Why do some caterpillars never make it, remaining forever a golden larva?

It is fair to say that, in reality, nobody is born with fully actualized talent. What differentiates some people from others has a lot to do with the way they take advantage of the opportunities given to them. Although each and every one of us may have a lot of inner potential, not everyone seems able to utilize their talents. Whether you can make the most of your different abilities, proclivities, and preferences depends very much on your developmental trajectory. Often, looking back at people's lives, what seems to be more important than innate capabilities is the environment into which they are born and the early experiences they have while growing up. The quality of these early experiences will shape the extent to which they are able to express and develop their innate skills and propensities. Childhood history can explain why some people are more effective in developing their potential than others.

Some know very well how to self-actualize; others, haunted by ghosts of the past, never become their best self.

Although each and every one of us may have a lot of inner potential, not everyone seems able to utilize their talents.

According to Abraham Maslow, "What a man can be, he must be. This need we call self-actualization."[1] It was Maslow in fact who coined the term "self-actualization," which can be defined as the psychological process whereby people maximize their abilities and resources through the pursuit of meaningful goals. There are multiple components to this process, including self-acceptance, creativity, spontaneity, autonomy, gratitude, empathy, compassion, and relationship satisfaction. Many people attempt to self-actualize but, in truth, few are able to succeed when complex psychological forces are holding them back.

FEAR OF FAILURE

A major reason why people find themselves stuck is an irrational but all-encompassing fear of failing, something that, in their inner world, they view as a catastrophe. Subsequently, they are afraid to take risks and prefer to defer or avoid entirely any activity or scenario that has the potential for an unsuccessful outcome. This may be the legacy of a previous failure; something that has left them with feelings of humiliation or shame. These negative emotions linger on, restricting the individual to perceived comfort zones, predictable environments, and habits. In this way they actively hold themselves back from potentially negative results but, as a consequence, they never realize their true potential.

With this outlook on life, these golden larvae may struggle with this anxiety—if there's any chance of failure, they won't attempt to achieve something. Not giving their best or following patterns of avoidance are ways of protecting themselves from potential embarrassment. Unfortunately, this approach to life can become a self-fulfilling prophecy; in fearing failure, these people are excluded from any real attempt or chance to become butterflies. If that's not tragic enough, this fear of failure can also contribute to a broad range of emotional and psychological problems, including feelings of anxiety, panic attacks, and depression. As the case of Stephen illustrates, fear of failure has a highly restrictive effect on how the individual performs at work, as well as how they interact with their friends and family members.

The original reason why people like Stephen act the way they do may well be associated with the environment in which they grow up. Perhaps from a young age they were taught that failure was unacceptable, and that anything less than "perfect" would be viewed as such. Unfortunately, this preoccupation with perfection comes at a high price—a constant nagging fear that one will never live up to these unrealistically high standards and will only ever disappoint. And all too easily this system of beliefs established in childhood can be carried into adulthood, resulting in a continual fear of making mistakes and living up to overly internalized high parental expectations even if the parents are no longer around.

Compounding this toxic psychological mix is that some of these people may have suffered abuse or severe punishment in early life if they failed to live up to what might well have been unrealistic expectations. Given these early experiences, their inner theater is occupied by feelings of shame, and they remain fearful of re-enacting those earlier scenarios.

In fact, there are many other possible explanations as to why people who fear failure might engage in acts of self-sabotage that undermine their chances of success.

FEAR OF SUCCESS

Fear of success can easily be confused with fear of failure, which is a difficult, seemingly contradictory concept to both identify and understand. There are, however, many reasons why people may be fearful of doing well. Some will be easy to grasp whereas others lurk beneath the surface. What people who fear success have in common, however, is that they are inclined to place obstacles in their own way, impairing their chances of doing well. These obstacles can range from minor acts of self-sabotage to more serious self-destructive behavior patterns that can come at great personal cost.

What should also be noted is that it isn't success itself that paralyzes these people but rather its consequences. It has less to do with fear and more to do with the changes that come with success, and whether an individual is ready for them. For example, these people may worry about the social repercussions of being too visible. They may find being in the spotlight extremely uncomfortable and feel anxious that they will not be able to handle all the attention. They may have additional self-limiting beliefs such as being unworthy of success.

Another reason these people may fear success is their concern that they will outshine other people whom they perceive to be equally or more deserving, creating feelings of guilt. Further to this, a fear of being criticized for "sticking out" and being a person others will be envious of may come to the fore. And, ironically, they worry that they will be soon be knocked off a pedestal that they may not have wanted to be on in the first place; that is, they worry about losing their success even after not wanting to be successful. Or, it may well be that these people fear that public success could lead to social or emotional isolation by alienating friends and leaving people behind.

These are some of the reasons why the realization of success provokes anxiety, self-doubt, and multiple negative concerns. And, although such worries are often hiding in the shadows, they all play a part in contributing to a person's self-sabotaging behavior.

Perfectionism could be another reason. As these people know that success may well come with heightened expectations, perfectionism could play an insidious role in this fear of success. As with the fear of failure, they may fear that they will be held to impossible standards that will only lead to disappointment, a worry that can prevent them from even trying to succeed. Common behavior patterns among these people will be delaying starting and/or completing a project. This kind of procrastination may result in missing an opportunity altogether or producing work of an indifferent quality.

Some people who fear success might also imagine that success will change them—and not necessarily for the better; that success, or earning a lot of money, will inflate their ego and turn them into different people. Such fears might encourage them to set the bar low in order to protect themselves from challenge, again possibly leading to acts of self-sabotage. One typical scenario is to find an excuse to quit just as they are on the verge of success. Worse, they may even engage in highly self-destructive behavior such as substance abuse that may derail them from being successful.

The root of these fears of success may again reside in childhood experiences, particularly in situations where a person has been belittled for success or scolded for showing it, leading them to avoid being in the spotlight whenever possible. Conversely, if as children their work went unacknowledged or was never deemed to be good enough, they might well become perfectionists in later life—a trait which, inherently, can be an invitation to failure. Childhood trauma of either nature can thus be the perfect setup for a fear of success that continues into adulthood.

IMPOSTERISM AND PETER PANISM

Imposterism

Woven into the fear of failure and the fear of success, you can also uncover themes such as imposterism and/or behaving like Peter Pan. The former refers to the feelings of self-doubt and personal incompetence that seem to plague these people, even in the face of success. Inevitably these self-proclaimed "impostors" live with a fear of being unmasked and carry the belief that they are presenting a "false self" to the external world.[2] Feelings of inauthenticity may leave them haunted by the idea that they are going to be exposed as a fraud. These feelings, however, are most likely "under the radar"; in other words, victims of imposter syndrome tend to suffer in silence. The reality is that they never feel good enough or capable of achieving the expectations placed upon them. Simply put, it is difficult for these people to recognize and celebrate their own strengths and accomplishments; they remain unable to objectively assess their competences and skills.

Of course, there is a certain self-fulfilling prophecy in the behavior of such people as, typically, they are very effective and well-practiced at putting themselves down, fearing what *could* happen. Again, as we have seen from those who fear either failure and/or success, these self-proclaimed "imposters" engage in acts of self-sabotage. Often, these people are convinced that their contributions will be sloppy, insufficient, or purposeless, and sending such messages to themselves on a continual basis can cause them to apply less effort, attention, creativity, and persistence to whatever task they are set, contributing to poor or risky decision-making. It is these negative core beliefs that ultimately hold them back from attaining their goals.

Once more, perfectionism may come into play. Some of these so-called impostors may think that every task that they tackle needs to be perfectly executed, and therefore carrying out a task becomes an impossible mission even before they begin. Whatever they do, they believe it will never be good enough. Even the experience of doing something well will do little to change this outlook on life. In fact, if they are successful, these people will tend to downplay their accomplishments. All too quickly, they will attribute their success to luck or other external factors. At the same time, this sense of being a fraud also compels them to constantly search for external validation. It is no wonder, therefore, that symptoms of anxiety and depression often accompany imposter syndrome—and perhaps even contribute to organizational burnout.

So how can we start to explain this pattern of behavior? It may well be that when these so-called impostors were growing up, their parents or other family members put excessive emphasis on achievement, or were overly critical, and thus, subsequently, their self-worth is explicitly connected to achievement. Such a developmental history contributes to a weak sense of self-esteem. What also seems to be the case is that people suffering from impostor syndrome often come from families where there have been high levels of conflict combined with low amounts of support.[3]

Peter Panism

Peter Pan syndrome is a term used to describe adults, usually men, who are reluctant to take on adult responsibilities in life. These people find it overly challenging to become productive members of society. For them, the emotional and financial responsibilities that come with adulthood are too overwhelming. Consequently, they prefer to hold on to their teenage years—a period when life appeared so much simpler. They prefer to continue living in Neverland, skirting the challenges that come with adulthood.

Clearly, these Peter Pans are reluctant to accept the fact that, at some point, everybody has to grow up, face real life, and make something of themselves. Instead, they cling to their childhood dreams and continue to experience the carefree days of their youth. With this outlook, they will always struggle to venture out on their own and will still demonstrate the childlike characteristics that most people leave behind when becoming adults. Instead, they prefer to depend on others (in particular, their parents) as a means of dealing with the vicissitudes of life.

Peter Pans don't appear to realize that their hold on such childhood dreams is unrealistic and that they are following a road with a dead end. They may exhibit low motivation, no interest in taking their work seriously, and evade accountability wherever possible. As exemplified in their behavior, they prove to be great procrastinators and tend to make excuses or blame others when things go wrong. They may be emotionally unstable and averse to personal growth, and they may even engage in abuse of drugs and alcohol.

Furthermore, Peter Pans typically experience a fear of commitment or avoid making decisions that necessitate adopting a position or taking a side. Rather than taking chances, they consider the safer alternative is to not commit, preferring to keep their options open and eschew making concrete plans. Unfortunately, this behavior—lack of effort, tardiness, or even the proclivity to skip work—jeopardizes their job. In many instances, they will move from field to field without developing any skills in a particular area.

Needless to say, this Peter-Pan-like behavior can only happen when enabled by others. What these enablers don't realize, however, is that by colluding with a Peter Pan, they are only sustaining his or her distorted worldview.

Again, an in-depth look at the childhood years may shed some light on the origins of such behavior. Peter Pans possibly had overly permissive or overprotective parents. In the case of the former, an overly permissive parenting style has allowed these children the freedom to do whatever they want with minimal consequences. By contrast, it could have been that they were brought up by overprotective, "helicopter" parents. They may have been told by their parents that the outside world is full of dangers. Consequently, to protect them, these parents took care of everything and so, as children, they weren't required to take any responsibility. Yet, without the opportunity to venture out on their own, overprotected children unsurprisingly become overly attached, insecure, and unable to develop the mindset or skills necessary for a successful transition into adulthood.

WAYS OF COPING

Returning to the case of Stephen, you can find elements of a number of these behavioral patterns—fear of failure, fear of success, and imposterism. Both the fear of success and the fear of failure seem to be playing a considerable role in making him a golden larva. In addition, feelings of imposterism also appear to contribute to his self-sabotaging behavior. We may even be able to see aspects of Peter Pan-like behavior. Whatever category people like Stephen may fall into, however, the likely outcome is that they are not going to become the best they can be. Clearly, Stephen isn't turning into a butterfly; he isn't self-actualizing and is therefore stuck in a larval stage, repeating certain self-destructive behaviors.

HOW TO BECOME A BUTTERFLY

Stephen's behavior may also raise questions for you. Do you recognize aspects of this persistent larval behavior in yourself?

If so, what can you do about it? What can you do to help yourself change into a butterfly?

The only way you can move forward is to understand what's keeping you back.

Understanding how your fears may be holding you back can be a huge obstacle, but it isn't one that can't be overcome. If you recognize some of these behavior patterns in yourself, you would do well to embark on a plan of action that might overcome this self-limiting behavior. It is time to tell another story about yourself. And to be able to do so, here are a number of action steps that you could take:

- *Acknowledge that you behave like a golden larva.* This is the first step in combating this form of self-destructive behavior. Only by acknowledging the presence of these dysfunctional behavior patterns and then working through the underlying issues that are holding you back will you be able to take the road to self-actualization. But, as a starter, you should realize that this self-sabotaging behavior will prevent you from living up to your full potential. The only way you can move forward is to understand what's keeping you back; this will mean confronting some of the deeply ingrained beliefs you are holding about yourself. You will need to acknowledge that something isn't right. You may be able to figure this out yourself or perhaps you will need someone else to encourage you to do some deep soul-searching.

  In the example of Stephen, it was his wife who encouraged him to seek help. When they married, she was full of hope for their future together. But having seen the repetitive setbacks in his career, she recognized that there was a destructive pattern to his behavior. Initially, Stephen rejected the idea that he had self-sabotaging tendencies, but he came to acknowledge that it was the case after she pointed out a number of incidents. Subsequently, she told him that he needed help. With my assistance, Stephen began to question whether his way of looking at life was realistic. After a considerable amount of self-reflection, he was able to trace his self-sabotaging activities back to events that happened in his childhood. Discovering these connections seemed to be quite an "aha!" experience for him. Furthermore, while we explored his past, he realized that various incidents in adulthood had added to his doubt about his capabilities. Either way, Stephen acknowledged that a major step in overcoming his compulsion to self-sabotage was to locate its root causes. To figure this out, I encouraged him to think about what kind of situations frightened him, reminding him that, while feelings were important, they would not always reflect reality.

In this context, while telling stories of people who have been in a similar situation, I encouraged Stephen to focus on the facts. I also pointed out that by separating feelings from facts—looking at the concrete and relevant data—he would be better equipped to determine how accurate or well-founded his feelings of self-doubt were. If, at any time, he discovered that being successful made him feel uncomfortable, he should allow himself some space to reflect on where that discomfort and its underlying imagery came from, and what they symbolized. This reflective process removed some of the immediate sting of emotion and helped him ascertain when his feelings were inflated or unfounded.

- *Reframe your thoughts.* I told Stephen stories of how people who had been in his situation had coped. I tried to make him understand that overcoming the tendency to self-sabotage would require a reframing of his experiences. This might mean viewing perceived past "failures" as positive opportunities for learning and growth. While engaging in this reflective process, I also suggested that he should try to experiment with this new way of looking at future challenges. It would help him to become a better version of himself. He should remind himself whenever possible that there is great power in the way he goes about looking at things.

What Stephen came to realize was that the way he looked at the world had the power to shape his reality in both positive and negative ways, just as the things he told himself could influence the way he saw himself. In fact, it became apparent that the difference between people who suffer from the golden larva syndrome and those who do not is in how they respond to the challenges they face. In Stephen's case, when negative thoughts popped into his head, he needed to start monitoring and modifying this inner voice. He needed to switch his self-sabotaging mindset by turning to more positive self-affirmations. And, even though these reframing actions do not lead to immediate results, clearly, over time, they would. To take such an approach also meant that Stephen needed to have a better understanding of his strengths and weaknesses. He needed to acknowledge what he was really good at. Effectively, he needed to identify not only the hidden benefits of past failures but also acknowledge his past successes. While, of course, there could be past events that would validate his fear of failure as well as success, Stephen had to acknowledge that these setbacks did not need to paralyze him. Instead, he should reframe failure as an opportunity for learning. By taking this route, he would come to feel more secure about himself.

It also became clear to Stephen that he should try *not* to compare himself with other people. I pointed out to him that if he cared too much about what others were thinking, failure would be just around the corner. Instead of comparing himself with others, he should focus on what he wanted to be like. And while in this comparison mode, I told him to remind himself that most people tend only to highlight the good things that have happened in their lives; rarely do they emphasize their failures. Far too many people are into image management and he shouldn't be fooled. Positive self-affirmations could help him pivot those unhelpful thoughts to empowering ones, which in turn could increase his sense of self-confidence.

- *Visualize all potential outcomes of the activities in which you are involved.* Helped by the telling of stories, Stephen came to realize that he could prevent golden larva behavior from coming to the fore by pausing to imagine multiple possible endings before acting. Such an exercise would encourage him to develop a vision of the life that he would like to have, and the steps he needed to take to realize this vision. In fact, by imagining himself doing well, he would feel more positive, which in turn could enhance his performance.

Conversely, as I pointed out to him, ruminating about what might go wrong would only provoke further anxiety, increasing the likelihood of the failure that Stephen feared could happen. Yet, having said this, he also came to realize that there were certain instances where it would be helpful to imagine a worst-case scenario in the grand scheme of his life. By doing so, he could then understand that the dreaded scenario wasn't going to be as terrible as he had presumed. He needed to discover that it was his fear of the unknown that was blocking him from moving forward. Thus, by going through these kinds of mental exercises, he could come to see that, even if things didn't turn out how he hoped, he would be okay in the end—if he did fail, it wouldn't be the end of the world. In this context, I reminded him of a comment once made by the Roman philosopher Seneca the Younger: "There is nothing so wretched or foolish as to anticipate misfortunes. What madness it is in your expecting evil before it arrives!"[4]

- *Let go of your inner perfectionist.* Stephen realized that he should practice setting himself challenging but realistic, and most importantly, achievable goals. Again, he needed to remind himself that mistakes are part of life, and that, if he didn't hit a particular goal or get something done on time, it wasn't going to be the end of the world. In fact, when he felt like a fraud, it was usually because he was trying to attain some perfect outcome that was either impossible or unrealistic. And thus, if he adjusted his standards for success, it would be easier for him to see and internalize his accomplishments. I pointed out to him that his challenge would be to cherish the term "good enough." Instead of beating himself up for falling short, he should learn from what had happened and move on, telling himself "I will be successful next time." In other words, he should focus on progression, not perfection. And when he didn't meet his own standards, he needed to resist the urge to see his failure as a catastrophe. Frankly speaking, he should make an effort to be nicer to himself, to avoid negative internal dialogue—"I'm not good enough" or "I'm a loser"— and to harness the power of positive self-talk. Clearly, a more optimistic outlook on life would enable Stephen to reduce his stress and anxiety levels.

Focus on progression, not perfection.

- *Stretch your courage muscle.* Stephen recognized that he shouldn't be an ostrich and bury his head in the sand when presented with challenging situations. He needed to face what he was most afraid of. I encouraged him to say "yes" to new opportunities. By forcing himself to do so, he would be undertaking a kind of "exposure therapy," a form of intervention that has frequently been found effective in dealing with phobias.

  To help Stephen in this desensitization process, I suggested that he made a list of all the ways he had been self-sabotaging his path to success. Making this list helped him to better understand what he was doing and brought what was holding him back into sharper focus. By embarking on this exercise, Stephen discovered that he no longer needed to fear mistakes. Instead, he learned enough from them to rise above these concerns. He realized that he had been turning down career-making opportunities because he didn't believe that he could do a good job. Gradually, Stephen realized that if he was prepared to face his fears, and be open to challenges, he would find it much easier to deal with them.

  Step by little step, Stephen was learning to see what he was up against as positive rather than negative. He was able to remind himself of the cost of not trying. He realized that by not taking up the challenge, he would miss out on some of life's great opportunities. Also, he came to appreciate that trying and failing was a much better option than not trying at all. Basically, he shouldn't let his inner larva turn down potentially game-changing opportunities. Gradually, he came to understand how, in the past, failure would all too often be the outcome if he delayed a decision in the hope that a bad situation was going to get better. Instead, he needed to be courageous. By doing so, he would be surprised what he could accomplish.

- *Celebrate your successes.* I also pointed out to Stephen that the next time he believed that he had done something well, he should make sure to celebrate his success. One of the best ways to manage and defeat the golden larva syndrome is to reflect on one's past successes and milestones. Therefore, it was important that Stephen owned his accomplishments and made a point of rewarding himself. He shouldn't just brush away his achievements but rather *truly* appreciate the role he had played in his own successes.

Encouraged by me, Stephen began to pay attention to his habit of engaging in negative self-talk. He learned not to fall back on excuses when he met with success, such as saying "I was just lucky." I suggested that he could even create a diary of his successes, both at work and in his personal life. This exercise enabled him to tell a much more constructive story about himself. Changing his inner monologue helped Stephen to cultivate a greater sense of self-compassion, to be kinder to himself. Increasingly, he practiced monitoring and modifying the way he talked to himself in his head. He realized that his negative self-talk was an unhealthy practice that would only increase his anxiety and stress levels. Instead, he made an effort to place kindness and compassion above severe self-criticism and self-doubt. He came to the realization that by acting in this manner, he could create a more realistic perspective of himself. Stephen was now able to remind himself that he was entitled to make mistakes—and, when he did, to forgive himself. He learned to tell himself that everyone fails. There was no need for self-flagellation, feeling guilty, or putting himself down. Instead, Stephen learned to talk to himself in a way that was more supportive, kind, and caring. He learned to accept the fact that mistakes were inevitable, but that he would do better next time.

- *Don't suffer in silence.* Stephen also came to see the importance of not bottling his feelings up. From our various exchanges, he had come to accept the benefits of asking for help (see Chapter 5).

He had come to realize what was blocking him from doing so and that he didn't have to do everything alone. He had found that confiding in people he trusted was helpful. And, as he had discovered, having these exchanges could also be quite cathartic.

Although there is something to be said about figuring out by yourself what's holding you back, at those times when the golden larva syndrome is taking the upper hand and threatening your everyday existence it is worthwhile to seek the help of someone close to you or even professional help. A coach or psychotherapist may assist you in understanding why you are fearful of personal achievement. Such a professional may also help you to appreciate your potential skills and accomplishments. In fact, sharing your feelings of self-doubt can be a powerful way of overcoming these concerns.

Assisted by a helping professional, you may come to realize the real limits and damage caused by acts of self-sabotage. With their support, you may no longer resort to such self-sabotaging behavior and begin to embrace the possibility of your success.

Importantly, by talking about your fears—either with a helping professional or someone you trust—you may come to realize that other people could also be suffering from this golden larva syndrome. And, like Stephen, you may discover that you are not alone in your predicament. Such a discovery may bring with it a sense of relief, making it easier to move on. Furthermore, if you realize that there are people in your life who only feed your fear of success, it can be beneficial to sit and talk with them. If they refuse to see how their actions are causing you harm, walk away and surround yourself with people who believe in you.

As it turned out, Stephen had been spending too much time with a toxic person—a university acquaintance for whom the glass was always half-empty. Interactions with this person did not bolster Stephen's self-image. Yet, when he reminded this person of this pattern of negativity—and how it would put a damper on any conversation—this person carried on doing what he had always done. This time, however, having acquired new insights about himself, Stephen decided that he would be much better off mood wise if in the future he limited his inter-actions with this person.

When you start to experiment with new ways of looking at the challenges you're facing, you will be setting out on a journey to become a better version of yourself.

Whenever that little voice in your head whispers that you're not good enough, you can whisper back that you're in the process of getting better. As the example of Stephen illustrates, when you start to experiment with new ways of looking at the challenges you're facing, you will be setting out on a journey to become a better version of yourself.

CONCLUDING THOUGHTS

Of course, for Stephen it was a real challenge to overcome his golden larva syndrome. But he had the courage to face his predicament and ask for help. Encouraged by me, he took the various steps mentioned above and gradually came to realize what he really had to offer. By facing his inner demons, he managed to actualize his full potential. Eventually, he was able to tell a better story about himself.

As an encouragement, I also told him to consider how famous people had overcome their inner and outer demons. Using various stories, I explained how disturbing experiences originating from childhood *can* be overcome. For example, purportedly, Beethoven had a music teacher who told him that he was hopeless as a com-poser; Thomas Edison (the inventor of the light bulb, the phono-graph, and the motion picture camera) was also regularly told as a child that he was too stupid to learn anything; and Albert Einstein was advised by his teacher to quit school because he would never amount to anything.

Finding ways of transcending personal concerns has proven to be a highly effective means to grow and evolve even further as an individual.

Clearly, people like Stephen can make the most of their lives if they can learn to stop self-sabotaging themselves and accept that being alive means trying to be the best that they can be. And while they are doing so—in the process or journey toward self-actualization—they could also think about contributing to something bigger than themselves. In fact, finding ways of transcending personal concerns has proven to be a highly effective means to grow and evolve even further as an individual. This "something bigger" could be a worthy cause, devoting time to community affairs, or simply helping a friend in need. These are all ways of applying personal qualities to make the world a better place. In that respect, Stephen would do well to consider the wisdom of the words of the Austrian psychiatrist and holocaust survivor, Victor Frankl: "Self-actualization is not an attainable aim at all … self-actualization is possible only as a side-effect of self-transcendence."[5] And after some encouragement, Stephen also paid heed to these words by spending time at a local orphanage, helping young people to develop themselves—an activity that gave him a great amount of satisfaction. In turn, it helped him to create a very different story for himself, and to spread his butterfly wings.

NOTES

[1] Abraham Maslow (1968). *Toward a Psychology of Being*. New York: Van Nostrand.

[2] Donald Winnicott (1965). "Ego Distortion in Terms of True and False-Self," in *The Maturational Process and the Facilitating Environment: Studies in the Theory of Emotional Development*. New York: International Universities Press. See also Pauline R. Clance and Susanne A. Imes (1978). "The Impostor Phenomenon in High Achieving Women: Dynamics and Therapeutic Intervention." *Psychotherapy: Theory, Research & Practice*, 15(3): 241–247.

[3] Joe Langford and Paulin Rose Clance (1993). "The Imposter Phenomenon: Recent Research Findings Regarding Dynamics, Personality and Family Patterns and Their Implications for Treatment." *Psychotherapy Theory Research Practice Training*, 30(3): 495–501.

[4] Seneca the Younger (1896 [c. 65 AD]). *The Cyclopedia of Practical Quotations*. Compiled by Jehiel Keeler Hoyt. New York: Funk & Wagnalls Company, Section: Misfortune, Quote Page 727, Column 1.

[5] Victor Frankl (1962). *Man's Search for Meaning*. Boston, MA: Beacon Press.

7

THE IDIOCY OF STUPIDITY

If a person is stupid, we excuse him by saying that he cannot help it; but if we attempted to excuse in precisely the same way the person who is bad, we should be laughed at.

—*Arthur Schopenhauer*

The world is so full of simpletons and madmen, that one need not seek them in a madhouse.

—*Johann Wolfgang von Goethe*

Sie reden doch jedenfalls von Dingen, die sie gar nicht verstehen. Ihre Sicherheit ist nur durch ihre Dummheit möglich.*

—*Franz Kafka*

HEAVEN AND HELL

The story has been told that even though many wise people cannot create heaven, it only takes one fool to create a hell on Earth. Clearly, giving power to a fool was something Prussian

---

* Translation: In any case, they're talking about things they don't even understand. Their safety is only possible because of their stupidity.

DOI: 10.4324/9781003508939-7

general Kurt von Hammerstein-Equord found particularly dangerous. Reflecting on the behavior of his soldiers, the story he told all who would listen to him was that he would divide them into four types: the clever, the industrious, the lazy, and the stupid.[1] According to his categorization, each soldier would always possess two of these characteristics. Having ascertained their personality makeup, the general's challenge was how to make the best use of his people. Thus, after an assessment, he would appoint the ones who were clever and industrious to the General Staff. The ones who were lazy and stupid (a cohort that the general estimated to make up 90 percent of an army) were, according to him, quite suited for routine duties—the infantry being an excellent area in which to place them. Soldiers who were clever and lazy were qualified to take on the highest leadership positions with the belief that they possessed the intellectual clarity and composure to deal with even the most complex issues. However, the soldiers the general was most wary of were the stupid and industrious. In fact, he believed this grouping to be extremely dangerous, to the extent that they shouldn't be entrusted with any responsibility, would always cause trouble, and should therefore be gotten rid of.

Even though many wise people cannot create heaven, it only takes one fool to create a hell on Earth.

Clearly, the general subscribed to the rule that what could easily be attributed to malice could also be reasonably explained by stupidity. He had learned that not only were stupid people dangerous but also that their behavior could be highly contagious. Like the expression that foolish sheep make wolves their confessors, he noted that foolish people had a potentially disturbing effect on others. Essentially, stupid people are safe to be stupid, as long as they keep their stupidity to themselves. When they begin to influence other people, however, they enter another dimension. Having learned from experience, it is clear that the general took human stupidity very seriously. He knew that stupid behavior could have catastrophic consequences.

Obviously, the general knew how to get people's attention by telling this story. He was also very concerned about the dangers of stupidity. As stupidity has many colors, this chapter will tell stories to help us understand what stupidity is all about, while the subsequent chapter will deal with what can be done about it.

Stupid people are safe to be stupid, as long as they keep their stupidity to themselves.

WHAT ARE STUPID PEOPLE LIKE?

You needn't look far to see that few things are more common than human stupidity. In fact, if we take an objective look at the world in which we live, we appear to be surrounded by people behaving stupidly—people who tell stupid stories. What's more, human folly is not limited to a select few. Most people, at one time or another, have acted stupidly. It is inevitable therefore that so many descriptors remain in circulation: stupidity, dumbness, silliness, obtuseness, imbecility, foolishness, folly, and idiocy, and so on. What such terms emphasize is that stupid people demonstrate their idiocy by embarking on remarkably stupid acts that inevitably make others aware of their stupidity.

What you also may discover is that these people seem to be incapable of properly navigating the domains of reasoning, planning, problem solving, abstract thinking, complex ideas, and learning from experience. However, what is troubling is that these people's actions are often devoid of mature judgment or reflective thinking.

An intelligent mask

An additional, rather disconcerting factor is that stupid acts are often committed by people who, at first glance, seem to be quite intelligent. Many highly intelligent, knowledgeable people have, in fact, been known to do extremely stupid things and with some regularity, things with the potential to be disastrous.

On the basis of such behavior, it appears that *real* stupidity can also be the hallmark of frightening intellectual complacency.

These individuals' lack of reflectivity is responsible for their stupid actions, although it is frequently the case that nobody labels people as complete idiots until the consequences of their actions prove them to be so. Only with the benefit of hindsight do others recognize that the people they have been dealing with were idiots all along. In other words, stupidity has a lot to do with the choices people make. Rational decision-making is not their forte.

Human folly is not limited to a select few.

Stubbornness

Another quality commonly seen in stupid people is stubbornness. All too frequently, they cling ardently to their opinions regardless of how off-track these may be. The Roman statesman and philosopher Marcus Cicero once commented on this personality characteristic when he said, "Every man is liable to err; it is the part only of a fool to persevere in error."[2] Unfortunately, it appears that these people don't realize *how* ignorant they really are—they engage in stupid acts with real self-assurance. This suggests that there may well be a narcissistic element to their behavior. And this, when in tandem with self-delusional patterns, is a mutually reinforcing combination, only binding the individual further to their behavioral habits—their state of stupidity.

An example of this might be if an individual were to be offered an exciting educational opportunity, only to decline it on the defeatist grounds that the program doesn't contain anything new. All too often, when life offers these people the possibility to grow, and change, they seem to be incapable of breaking free of their old habits. Instead, and arguably stupidly, they prefer to hang on to the tried and tested, instead of the new and exploratory.

Another example of stupidity, this time in the political domain, might be a situation whereby a group of people believe that one party (of course, their party) is utterly virtuous and indisputably correct on specific issues, while the other party is viewed as completely evil and always wrong. Obviously, such people are unable to accept shades of gray and incapable of considering an alternative perspective. In such cases, stupid people lack the mental resources that might allow them to recognize their own imbecility. Unfortunately, we may discover the hard way that most fools deny their own foolishness and underestimate their stupidity.

Most fools deny their own foolishness and underestimate their stupidity.

Pseudo-stupidity

What should also be addressed here is that there may be such a thing as pseudo-stupidity, referring to people who deliberately behave stupidly for ulterior motives, most usually to mislead others and get what they want. There are many instances in which smart people who don't want to stand out opt to "play dumb" as a way of staying under the radar.

HUMAN STUPIDITY MAKES THE WORLD GO ROUND

Fundamentally, humans have seldom been known for their wisdom; on the contrary, the history of humankind has always been a struggle between wisdom and stupidity. As William Shakespeare wrote, "Lord, what fools these mortals be."[3] Or to quote the German humanitarian Albert Schweitzer, "Man is a clever animal who behaves like an imbecile."[4] What is most worrisome—reflecting on the history of humanity—is that stupidity has a knack of repeating itself. Calamity after calamity occurs when we, the human race, should have learned from recent history and known how to avoid destructive actions.

What maintains stupidity in humans is actually the very same thing that has allowed our evolution—the pervasive desire to explain the inexplicable. Throughout our evolution, history has exposed humans to many dangers, and people have always sought explanations for events perceived to be mysterious. In these situations, the very bizarre stories told to offer explanations for strange phenomena prompt irrational beliefs that frequently overrule rationality. Furthermore, as a species, humans are both anxiety-prone and gullible. This means we are experts at transmitting both anxiety and irrationality to others.

Fundamentally, humans have seldom been known for their wisdom.

Touch wood and lucky numbers

Some humans seem only too willing to believe the craziest ideas, so much so that others may question their sanity. In an effort to make sense of the world, some individuals might consult horoscopes, visit psychics, believe in the miracles of Chinese alternative medicinal treatments, advocate homeopathic cures, explore black magic and voodoo, or believe in ghosts, spirits, demons, and angels. Some repeatedly search out "lucky" numbers for the lottery, fear walking under ladders or opening umbrellas indoors; others swear by palm reading or knock on wood for good luck—all repetitive behaviors and beliefs of puzzling origin and purpose.

What is more, human beings are particularly susceptible to conjuring retrospective explanations, making up the kind of stories that prove them right. They then continue to hold on to their strange beliefs regardless of the price they may pay or the harm they may inflict. Particular modes of magical thinking come to the fore when pursuing big ideas of the kind upheld by many religious movements, ideologies, and cults. Although some of the stories behind these ideologies and religious orientations can provide great comfort to people, they also tend to negate any form of rationality. Thus, although all of us may be prone to a certain degree of idiocy, ideologically driven people show more of this tragic quality—and the superstitious, in particular, are led by it.

It is no wonder that ideologies have been referred to as "the science of idiots," or, to quote the American science fiction writer Isaac Asimov, "There is no belief, however foolish, that will not gather its faithful adherents who will defend it to death."[5] Again, what the obstinate persistence of strange beliefs proves is that no human being is immune from or unfamiliar with some kind of absurd belief system. In fact, anxiety prone as people tend to be, they are always searching for some form of causality and meaning. In the context of humanity, logical delirium seems to be ever present.

As a species, humans are both anxiety prone and gullible.

THE QUESTION OF LIMITED RATIONALITY

Being a complex and controversial subject, stupidity has been explored from any number of different angles. It has garnered significant interest from philosophers, sociologists, and psychologists, in particular. Taking the perspective of psychologists, stupidity has often been looked at as the outcome of cognitive biases or errors in judgment.[6] In fact, most of the explanations given by prominent psychologists refer to *Homo sapiens'* cognitive limitations, deeming these to be a causal factor for beliefs that defy rational logic and lead to stupid actions.

Fortunately, research on human cognition and decision-making has helped us to better understand the reasons why such strong biases occur. These findings have made it clear that people are anything but rational, optimizing machines. As Herbert Simon, a winner of the Nobel Prize for economics, concluded, humans have significant limitations in the context of rationality.[7] Daniel Kahneman, the Israeli psychologist and yet another Nobel Prize winner, corroborated this, and observed that people think fast and slow—meaning fast, intuitive thinking, and slow, rational thinking—depending on the situation.[8]

Neuroscientists have also joined the fray, identifying that the frontal lobes of our brain (the source of rational thinking) are easily overruled by the more primitive mechanism of the amygdala—the core of the neural system needed for processing threatening stimuli.[9] Essentially, this differentiation between fast and slow decision-making implies that there are situations when slow, deliberate information processing will be inappropriate. In emergency situations, when faster decision-making is required, those slow, more calculated decision-making processes are overruled. But long before cognitive psychologists and neuroscientists studied such patterns, the French writer François Duc de La Rochefoucauld noted that "Passion often renders the most clever man a fool, and even sometimes renders the most foolish man clever."[10]

Cognitive biases

With these decision-making differences in mind, one cognitive bias frequently observed in relation to stupid behavior is the *confirmation bias*. We tend to favor information that confirms our pre-existing beliefs or hypotheses while ignoring or dismissing contradictory information. Another regularly occurring cognitive bias that could lead us astray in the context of decision-making is *anchoring*, meaning that we are often influenced by the first piece of information that we receive (the "anchor") when we make decisions, even when this information turns out to be completely irrelevant or arbitrary.

We tend to favor information that confirms our pre-existing beliefs or hypotheses while ignoring or dismissing contradictory information.

Furthermore, human beings are prone to the *overconfidence effect*, in which we overestimate our abilities, knowledge, and the accuracy of our beliefs. In other words, even though things may not turn out the way we expect, we fail to see that what happens is the result of our *own* actions. Not only this, but stupid people also fail to recognize competence in other people.

The *fundamental attribution error* is also relevant here. This happens when people attribute the behavior of others to internal factors (e.g., personality) rather than to external factors (e.g., situational influences) in an effort to make sense of apparently idiotic behavior.

Another explanation for stupid decisions is *groupthink*, when groups of people value consensus and conformity over critical evaluation—another bias that contributes to flawed decision-making.

Other biases include the *sunk cost fallacy*, when people continue to invest time, money, or resources in a project or endeavor past the point where it makes sense, and the *availability heuristic*, when people rely on readily available information, even when it is unrepresentative or even statistically inaccurate. In other words, people can see causality where there is no correlation.

All these various cognitive biases are means by which we simplify decision-making, enabling us to make quick decisions in stressful situations. Again, from an evolutionary perspective, our prehistoric ancestors, who lived at a time when quick decisions could mean the difference between life and death, were conditioned to respond quickly. Slow deliberation could be deadly. They were inclined to take action, any kind of action, based on the stories told to them, however appropriate or otherwise idiotic such an activity turned out to be. Consequently, we still exhibit all the responses of that evolutionary legacy where, at any point in time, fearful situations can make complete idiots out of us. All too easily, we are triggered to give a flight or fight response—an archaic behavior pattern seen over and over again in our contemporary society.

Of course, with this greater knowledge of such primitive cognitive limitations, we should recognize that, in many contexts, these biases are not entirely indicative of genuine stupidity. Rather, they are the result of cognitive tendencies to which we are all susceptible. But it is also arguable that the degree of insight now available should make us more aware of our own cognitive biases, especially given that they can be the source of personal misery. Unfortunately, despite cognitive stupidity being something we all have in common, there are those who insist they are entitled to improve on it.

STUPIDITY IN THE DIGITAL AGE

As this brief historical overview might suggest, when it comes to stupidity, people appear to have a very slow learning curve. The journey toward stupidity seems to be never-ending. In fact, ours might be considered the golden age of stupidity and, thanks to the explosive rise of social media, human follies have become more visible than ever. People who you might only have suspected of idiocy may now be giving you ample evidence, as the Italian writer Umberto Eco points out:

> Social media gives legions of idiots the right to speak when they once only spoke at a bar after a glass of wine, without harming the community ... but now they have the same right to speak as a Nobel Prize winner. It's the invasion of the idiots.[11]

Social media seems to be promoting stupidity, and, given the stories that they tell, too many journalists have turned into megaphones for it. Many of the people who contribute to these technological platforms are broadcasting at best inane, but often stupid, ideas. It is unfortunate that so many people are ready to believe them without question.

In this respect, we are living in something of a "post-truth" era. We are faced daily with the kind of public discourse that is difficult to distinguish as fact or fantasy. All too easily, we may be fooled by errors and lies, to the extent that the fake world is at risk of replacing the real, and with the added tool of simplistic but potent slogans intended to maximize the "engagement factor." In essence, those who control the media try to reach as many people as possible in the spread of their nonsensical ideas. They know that the way to increase this engagement factor is to present outrageous information. It is no wonder that these social media platforms have become the ideal outlet to tell stories imbued with cultish beliefs and behavior—niche cultures, spawning conspiracy theories that rapidly become mainstream ideas.

Group psychology

From a macro perspective, we should never underestimate the influence that one stupid individual can have. With our instinctual tendency toward herd behavior, we will quickly mimic the people around us. As touched upon earlier, stupidity in such contexts can be highly contagious and potentially dangerous. As the American polymath Benjamin Franklin once said, "Fools make feasts and wise men eat 'em."[12]

In the company of fools, you too may become a fool.

Groupthink reduces the human capacity for balanced judgment—in the company of fools, you too may become a fool. And when a large number of people embrace an idiotic theory, it is likely that others will be compelled to conform. In these kinds of situations, the whole certainly isn't greater than the sum of its parts. Even the most ordinary, good-hearted, intelligent people may begin to believe blatantly nonsensical ideas. And they start to spread these ideas within the stories they tell. Consequently, you must pause to reflect on whether you are ruled by smart people pretending to be idiots or by fools who really mean what they say.

Despite being aware of all this, people underestimate the number of stupid individuals in our midst. What's more, when wealth and power are at stake, the potential for stupidity is magnified. Whether people are following the antics of social media influencers such as Paris Hilton and Kim Kardashian or were seduced by the idea of instant riches through bitcoin encouraged by the likes of Samuel Bankman-Fried, stupidity seems to be celebrated. Clearly many foolish people are addicted to attention, fame, money, power, and prestige. Values we once considered to be commonsense have been replaced by sheer idiocy.

More troublesome still is the fact that critical thinking has become both a liability and a threat. Not only can you observe a proliferation of stupidity—celebrity cultures that embrace the banal and the idiotic—a similar phenomenon seems to be occurring in the discourses and policies of people in leadership positions. It is as if these individuals believe that the legacy of the Enlightenment—typified by ideas of liberty, progress, toleration, fraternity, and constitutional government—is due a reversal.

Presently, you can observe how people in an increasing number of countries are being incited, through the stories they are told, to follow the most stupid ideologies, irresponsible political parties, and strange social movements—activities often driven by media-savvy politicians. And many of these politicians are propagating utter nonsense. The weird, the stupid, and the coarse have become the new cultural norms and, perhaps, for many, even the new cultural ideals. More worrying still, the fools who are spreading these crazy ideas seem to believe their own lies and, despite their obvious stupidity, many people are taken in by their antics, lock, stock, and barrel.

You must pause to reflect on whether you are ruled by smart people pretending to be idiots or by fools who really mean what they say.

Inciting stupidity

Compounding the problem is the fact that the human species, haunted by its many fears and unintelligible fantasies, has always been at the mercy of people placed in leadership positions. From their position of power these individuals have reserved the right to do the thinking for the rest of society. As the people who follow them seem to be prepared to abdicate personal responsibility, it comes as no great surprise that much of the world's misery stems from mass stupidity. People listen mindlessly to the stories that these leaders spread, no matter how demagogue-like their ideas turn out to be. We don't need to go far to recognize many crazy activities driven by idealism, dogmatism, and a proselytizing zeal on behalf of religious or political fools. People's willingness to subscribe to these leaders' crazy ideas has contributed to a great deal of human suffering.

The combination of power and stupidity has always been a heady and dangerous mix. All too often, the foolish behavior of these demagogue-like leaders upends the lives of large numbers of people. A horrendous illustration is currently in action in the form of the Ukrainian war instigated by a remarkably stupid leadership decision. And similar comments can be made about the Gaza catastrophe. The human suffering on both sides of the divide has been immense. Yet, as long as there are stupid people supporting stupid leaders, the people living in those countries seemingly have little choice but to continue swimming in the cesspool created by their own foolishness. As this phenomenon occurs over and over again, it may explain why feelings of despair about the future of humankind will be inevitable.

A leadership tragedy

Another example of the contagiousness of stupidity among those in power, is the playbook of Donald Trump, the former president of the United States. Given the present political scene in the United States, he could perhaps be considered as the leading voice of stupidity, despite heavy competition from other political figures around the world. The question when considering all these types of leaders is who is more foolish—the fool or the people who follow them? What is quite clear, however, is that fools can always find greater fools to admire them. In this respect, Trump is one good example of stupidity working overtime, of a person telling foolish stories, with mind-baffling results.

Unfortunately, the media and supposedly intelligent people are complicit in a leader's rise to power and often encourage his or her outrageous behavior. As a result, people's fight–flight reactions are triggered, which doesn't always make for rational behavior. As leaders such as Trump have discovered and exploited, when people believe that the world is heading off a cliff, they become especially receptive to their siren songs and their stories will thus have a highly receptive audience.

In taking on the mantle of the populist-demagogue, such leaders, including Trump, are preaching doctrines that even *they* may realize to be untrue to people they deem gullible enough. Of course, through their constant reiteration it is quite possible these leaders are beginning to believe their own lies. Unfortunately, whatever the reality may be, the outstanding thing is that so many people keep on supporting their foolish antics. If an idiot were to tell you the same story every day for a year, might you end up believing it too? Taking the example of Trump, through his theatrics, he has been able to dumb down a large segment of the US population. Many people have been transformed into cult members. Unfortunately, they don't realize that they are all being taken for fools who are partaking in an act of mass stupidity.

Tragically, the number of people who harness the power of mass stupidity on a dangerous level seems to be increasing across the world. As masters of manipulation and persuasion, some current leaders and people in power possess a Pied Piper-like magic that enables them to call the tune, confident in the knowledge that many people will follow their lead. They have learned how to seduce their audiences, skilled as they are in using the people's wish to believe in whatever the nonsense they're preaching.

This political merry-go-round demonstrates the power of group dynamics, and how easily people can be swayed by the persuasive tactics of charismatic figures. Due to these psychological dynamics, given the kinds of stories they tell, leaders of this ilk will be able to exploit the psychological dynamics of a people whose judgment has become clouded by emotional factors that limit their cognitive capabilities. Consequently, the followers of these leaders conform to group actions, even when these actions are "stupid," and even contrary to their own best interests. In the meantime, such leaders present a stage spectacle full of myths and magic to their public, catering to their individual and collective fantasies with persuasive charisma.

In this respect, it cannot be emphasized enough how troubling it is that leaders have the qualities and tactics to seduce people left, right, and center. They have a position of responsibility that can lead people from a place where they were once serene into a world of agitation, where they are compelled to partake in frenzied rallies, to listen to endless lies, and to contribute their money to crooked causes. Yet, as perhaps Trump illustrates, it is the person who speaks the loudest, the person who conveys the most conviction and passion, who rules the roost. Passion not only makes idiots of the cleverest people, but also makes the biggest idiots look clever. Clearly, current political shenanigans demonstrate that you should never underestimate the appeal of stupidity, particularly not when delivered with absolute conviction. In fact, the German political satirist Karl Kraus emphasized this point when he said, "The secret of the demagogue is to appear as dumb as his audience so that these people can believe themselves as smart as he."[13] Many followers fail to realize that their participation in such *folie des masses* (group insanity) is an invitation to disaster. As Napoleon Bonaparte once put it, "In politics, an absurdity is not an impediment."[14]

By signing up for stupidity, people converted by these leaders' foolish messages forget that, in today's world, the dangers of making stupid decisions have become much greater, and the stakes higher. After all, it only takes one fool with a red button and a case of abject stupidity to eradicate the whole world as we know it. Consequently, given the stupidity of more and more of our contemporary leaders, the civil world as we know it is fragile. This must be at the forefront of our minds when we ignore or fail to question stupidity. All too quickly, it can evolve into malice.

Stupid people should be considered the most dangerous animals on Earth!

A personality recipe for disaster

Clearly, there is nothing funny about these leaders. Often, they turn out to be people without empathy, individuals who can be extremely vindictive, manipulative, and exploitative. In this respect, they exhibit many malignant narcissistic qualities—a disorder that can be defined as the most severe form of narcissism. In fact, the malignant narcissist has a more pervasive lack of empathy than would be the case for someone who merely possesses narcissistic characteristics. Aside from demonstrating grandiosity and superiority, these people also lack feelings of guilt or remorse for the damage they may cause.[15] Stupidity combined with arrogance, egotism, and vindictiveness is what encourages these people to do what they are doing.

Naturally, when it comes to a leader's idiotic campaigns and actions, you should always ask yourself whether this person is really stupid or whether they just *pretend* to behave stupidly to satisfy their own needs. In other words, are they just wearing a mask of stupidity to hide their rampant narcissism? Or to quote the Greek philosopher Heraclitus, "Stupidity is better kept a secret than displayed."[16] Still, whatever the situation, never underestimate the power of stupidity. Stupid people should be considered the most dangerous animals on Earth!

NOTES

1   Translation of the *Truppenführung*, the German Army field manual, https://commons.wikimedia.org/w/index.php?title=File:Truppenf%C3%BChrung_translation_by_United_States_Army.pdf&page=2

2   Marcus Cicero (1926 [March, 43 BC]). *Philippics*. Translated by Walter C. A. Ker. Cambridge, MA: Harvard University Press, Philippic 12. II. 5.

3   William Shakespeare (1595). *A Midsummer Night's Dream*. Puck, Act III, Scene ii.

4   Goodall, Jane (2007[2005]) "Reasons for Hope". In Valone, D. A. (ed.), *Reverence for Life Revisited: Albert Schweitzer's Relevance Today*. Transcript of an address given before the faculty, students, and staff of Quinnipiac University at the opening of the conference "Albert Schweitzer Reconsidered in October 2005." London: Cambridge Scholars.

5   Isaac Asimov (1971 [August 1970]). *The Stars in Their Courses*. New York: Doubleday, p. 36.

6   Dan Arieli (2009). *Predictably Irrational, Revised and Expanded Edition: The Hidden Forces That Shape Our Decisions*. New York: HarperCollins.

7   Herbert Simon (1947). *Administrative Behavior: A Study of Decision-Making Processes in Administrative Organizations*. New York: MacMillan.

8   Daniel Kahneman (2012). *Thinking Fast and Slow*. New York: Penguin.

9   Rupa Gupta, Timothy R. Koscik, Antoine Bechara, and Daniel Tranel (2011). "The Amygdala and Decision-making." *Neuropsychologia*, 49(4), 760–766.

10 François Duc de La Rochefoucauld (1871 [1665]). *Reflections; or Sentences and Moral Maxims*. Translated by J. W. Willis Bund and J. Hain Friswell. London: Simpson, Low, Son, and Marston, Maxim 6.

11 Nicoletti, G. (11 June 2015). "Umberto Eco: 'Con i social parola a legioni di imbecilli.'" *La Stampa (The Press)*. Turin.

12 Richard Saunders [Benjamin Franklin] (May 1733). *Poor Richard, 1733. An Almanack for the Year of Christ 1733*. Philadelphia, PA: B. Franklin.

13 Karl Kraus (1976). *Half Truths & One-and-a-Half Truths*. Karl Kraus: Selected Aphorisms. Quebec: Engendra Press.

14 Jules Bertaut (ed.) (1916). *Napoleon in His Own Words*. Translated by Herbert Edward Law and Charles Lincoln Rhodes. Chicago, IL: McClurg & Co, p. 38.

15 Manfred F. R. Kets de Vries (2021). *Leadership Unhinged: Essays on the Ugly, the Bad, and the Weird*. London: Palgrave MacMillan.

16 Heraclitus (2003 [c. 500 BC]). *Fragments*. Translated by Brooks Haxton. Harmondsworth, UK: Penguin, fragment 109, p. 82.

8

BEYOND STUPIDITY

Inhumanity is the keynote of stupidity in power.

—Alexander Berkman

Speech is great; but Silence is greater.

—Thomas Carlyle

On the Internet you can be anything you want. It's strange that so many people choose to be stupid.

—Anon.

TO HELL WITH STUPIDITY

To continue our storytelling journey, as mentioned previously, the overriding question this chapter tries to address is whether anything can be done in dealing with people who behave stupidly. Given their story, can these people be converted? If that's what we set out to do, it must be with an understanding of the challenge to follow. In fact, many people have written it off as a hopeless task. For example, the Bible says, "A fool finds no pleasure in understanding but delights in airing his own opinions."[1] After this,

DOI: 10.4324/9781003508939-8

in 1801, the German playwright Friedrich Schiller stated, "Against stupidity, the very gods themselves contend in vain."[2] What's clear is that many people believe that no amount of persuasion will ever transform an idiot. After all, much of the time you may be dealing with people who are completely unaware of their idiocy. Based on their levels of conviction, forcing a stupid person to accept a different perspective will be out of the question, and the accusation of idiocy deflected.

LESS IS MORE

In the context of cognitive biases that we touched upon in the previous chapter, it has been said that the less people know, the more certain they are that they are right. On this premise it is no wonder that the people who hang on to stupid ideas are so resolute. For them, changing their opinion is not an option. The American poet James Russell Lowell sadly concurred with this tendency, saying, "The foolish and the dead alone never change their opinions."[3] It is exactly this overconfidence that makes such individuals so difficult to deal with, and all the more so when in tandem with narcissistic behavior. As these people thrive on power and control, they defend their position and deny foolishness, regardless of innumerable counterarguments. Instead, they will project their stupidity onto other people, or to quote Euripides, "Talk sense to a fool and he calls you foolish."[4]

The less people know, the more certain they are that they are right.

In fact, you may have discovered that reasoning with an idiot can be as bewildering as it is frustrating. Most often, it will fall on deaf ears and the discussion will go nowhere. To argue against stupidity only seems to reinforce it. Worse still, the more you try to reason with these people, the stronger they seem to get. Facts that contradict personal prejudices will simply be ignored. Arguments that are presented to show that they are wrong will be plainly denied. Instead, fools will try to adjust the truth so that *they* don't have to adjust their opinions or change the stories they tell. Any evidence that suggests they are wrong will be pushed aside or looked upon as trivial exceptions. These people are practicing what can be called "whataboutism," whereby a critical question is not explored but responded to with a critical counter-question. These defensive responses suggest such people despise real understanding and sound knowledge; they can be almost unteachable, uncoachable, and even proud of their own ignorance. In dealing with these people, rational discourse may have no effect. What is also notable is that in conversation, in the stories they tell, they do not appear as *real* people but are made up of slogans and catchwords, spellbound and immune to hard facts. They are blinded by their ignorance.

To argue against stupidity only seems to reinforce it.

"WE SHALL FIGHT ON THE BEACHES"[5]

Despite the mounting challenges, efforts still need to be made to counteract stupidity. You should not abandon all hope of being able to reason with these people—to try to change their storyline. To patiently accept stupidity, in light of the possible outcomes, isn't really an option. Given stupidity's contagiousness, ways need to be found to deal with such behavior. Regimes like Hitler's Nazi Germany, Maoist China, and Pol Pot's Cambodia have shown that a country has a tremendous amount to lose when its leaders force an idiotic personal vision onto a society. Presently, a similar replay of these demagogue-disasters is taking place in many areas of the world. One prominent example is Russia, where Putin and his inner circle seem to be actively telling stories to dumb down the Russian population, almost relying on "stupidity" to censor stark reality and factuality through, among other things, self-deception and lies.

Institutional measures

To persuade these people of the errors of their ways, however, is not without risks. Often, it takes very little for them to behave aggressively, and for this exact reason, it becomes even more pressing to take action.

Taking a societal point of view, a major countervailing power against stupidity is the presence of institutional safeguards. The citizens of a country need to make great efforts to create a strong civic culture. They need to establish a society in which people will be able to influence their government and have their voices heard in many different ways. In particular, a strong independent judiciary is a means of establishing boundaries against idiotic behavior. To take a very recent example from the United States, you can see how this boundary-setting process is working overtime to negate the result of Trump's participation in the presidential election.

Further legislation will be needed to discourage these individuals from disseminating misinformation. There should be some legal recourse to prevent the spread of fake news. If false facts cause personal damage, if stories defy reality, the victims of these activities should be able to bring defamation suits and their efforts to do so supported.

Perhaps most importantly, measures must to be taken to prevent people from falling victim to conspiracy theories. Unfortunately, given the difficulties in defining what's permissible, tackling disinformation in today's world can be quite a challenge. Most importantly, however, whatever steps are taken in creating these laws, the greatest efforts should always be made to protect the freedom of speech.

Satire

Satire may sound like an unlikely countermeasure in the battle against stupidity. However, the use of absurdity can be a powerful way of challenging foolish ideas. Witty humor has the potential to prompt reflection and critical thinking, ideally without being insulting or offensive. In fact, satire can be most effective when directed at powerful institutions, policies, public figures, or stupid ideologies. Its focus should be on critiquing ideas, beliefs, and actions rather than attacking people personally. It should be seen as a springboard for reflection on major policy issues—a way to question assumptions.

In this sense satire as an educational tool could be a highly effective intervention to help stupid people question their logic. Hopefully, it will encourage them to adopt a more self-critical form of reasoning on what could be the start of an educational journey. The challenge is to tell the kinds of stories that help people develop a consciousness of their ideological limitations. However, such a discourse needs to be handled with a great deal of respect and empathy. To go head to head with people who hold idiotic ideas is not the answer.[6] Instead, it is advisable to use constructive reasoning, provide evidence, and engage in clear communication. Personal attacks or condescension will not make for very meaningful communication. Rather, there might be merit in adopting a more judo-like approach and "bend with the resistances" (see Chapter 3) when trying to convince these people to accept alternative points of view.

Paradoxical intervention

Another way to deal with stupidity will be to resort to paradoxical intervention. Instead of being told to avoid specific stupid activities, the person could be encouraged to do more of them.[7] The aim of this somewhat risky strategy is to have them see the errors of their way and should be a last resort. Counterintuitive though it sounds, the challenge is to allow people to have their own way. When their activities lead to disastrous results, hopefully their foolishness will become self-evident. The expectation is that they will learn from the experience and understand that their singular view may not be completely right or clear. Even though it may be difficult for them to choose between right and wrong, it will, most likely, be less difficult to choose between sensible and stupid. The disastrous result of their actions could be an eye-opener, causing a modicum of doubt about the wisdom of their ways— doubt can be a highly effective antidote to stupidity. Thus, in the context of decision-making and judgment it will be important to have these people understand that everyone has both strengths and weaknesses—themselves included.

General education

There is always the possibility of a more general educational effort, difficult as such an undertaking can be. Simply put, educating people about the relevant issues could be an intervention that prevents stupid actions. It could be a way of counteracting excessive self-assurance and arrogance through a personal discovery of their ignorance. As Confucius once said, "When you know a thing, maintain that you know it; and when you do not, acknowledge your ignorance. This is characteristic of knowledge."[8] In this respect, a thriving education system will be an important countervailing force against stupidity.

In the context of knowledge management, efforts could also be made to mitigate the effects of cognitive biases. Such a learning journey can be seen as yet another form of intervention. In fact, working on critical thinking skills and training in decision-making can go a long way toward counteracting stupidity. If these people recognize their cognitive biases, they may be more willing to contribute to productive discussions and gain greater insights into their behavior. Clearly, ignorant people need to be taught how to properly decode the information they deal with. They need to figure out whether their own observations and those of others are really evidence-based. The challenge is to make them more reflective. Of course, to help them get to this point will require greater data transparency and fact-checking to help them recognize all that is wrong in their deluded beliefs.

Self-knowledge: a virtuous cycle

Self-knowledge can be the greatest antidote to stupidity. When people acquire a modicum of self-knowledge, it enables them to reflect on their foolish behavior more objectively. They may come to realize, after so long insisting they are surrounded by fools, that it is in fact *they* who are the real idiots. What they label as foolishness in others may turn out to be their own ignorance. In this respect, stupidity can be seen as a resistance to logic, or the result of a poverty of mind.

When people acquire a modicum of self-knowledge, it enables them to reflect on their foolish behavior more objectively.

In this chapter I have highlighted situations in which stupidity might be understood as a condition of self-idolatry, discernible particularly in individuals with narcissistic tendencies. It demonstrates that these people may be too full of themselves, that they aren't really interested in the opinions of other people. Such individuals need to obtain a more reality-based view on life and a capacity for self-criticism. With self-criticism comes the ability to be empathic—another strong antidote against stupidity—or, to quote the French artist Paul Gauguin, "We never really know what stupidity is until we have experimented on ourselves."[9] Given the human tendency to externalize one's internal theater—something many leaders tend to do, with consequences that impair the lives of a wider audience—in the public sphere, self-criticism becomes even more important.

Generally speaking, an effective leader, whether in government, business, or any other sector, requires a combination of intelligence, knowledge, wisdom, empathy, and compassion. Additional qualities that qualify leaders to make informed decisions on the betterment of society include the capacity for critical thinking, to have problem-solving skills, to be capable of dealing with complex issues, to have the ability to collaborate with others, and—most significant in this context—the ability to differentiate between fools and other people. We need leaders who have the capability to weave these qualities into the stories they tell. Such leaders may not be able to entirely prevent people falling victim to crazy beliefs, but they can lead by example—one that is wildly different from that demonstrated by idiotic leaders.

LIGHT AT THE END OF THE TUNNEL

This exploration of stupidity is not all doom and gloom. In fact, in the eighteenth century, English poet and hymnodist William Cowper made the reassuring statement that "A fool must now and then be right by chance."[10] Perhaps we might even infer a counterargument from this: that there are times when we actually *need* some individuals to behave stupidly—to have some people to tell seemingly stupid stories. After all, history has demonstrated that it has often been the court fool, not the foolish courtier, who proved most adept in preventing foolish people from losing their heads!

NOTES

[1] *The New International Bible*, Proverbs 18 verse 2.
[2] Friedrich Schiller (1899 [1801]). *Die Jungfrau von Orleans [The Maid of Orleans]*. Translated by Anna Swanwick. Philadelphia, PA: David McKay, Act III, Scene vi.
[3] James Russell Lowell (1871). *My Study Windows*. Cambridge, MA: Welch, Bigelow & Co, p. 166.
[4] Euripides (1959 [405 BC]). "The Bacchæ." In David Grene and Richmond Lattimore (eds.), *Euripides V*. Translated by William Arrowsmith. The Complete Greek Tragedies. Chicago, IL: University of Chicago Press.
[5] Winston Churchill. Speech in the House of Commons (4 June 1940). Hansard HC Deb 4 June 1940 vol 361 cc787–98.
[6] Manfred F. R. Kets de Vries (2023). "How to Change Someone's Mind." INSEAD Knowledge: https://knowledge.insead.edu/leadership-organisations/how-change-someones-mind
[7] L. Michael Ascher (2002). "Paradoxical Intention," *Encyclopedia of Psychotherapy*, edited by M. Hersen and W. Sledge (vol. 2, pp. 331–338). Cambridge, MA: Academic Press.
[8] Confucius (475–221 BC). In Epiphanius Wilson (ed.) (1900). "The Analects of Confucius." In *Chinese Literature: Comprising the Analects of Confucius, the Shi-King, the Sayings of Mencius, the Sorrows of Han, and the Travels of Fa-Hien*. Section translated by William Jennings. London: The Colonial Press, Book II.
[9] Paul Gauguin (1921). *Gauguin's Intimate Journals*. Translated by Van Wyck Brooks. New York: Boni & Liveright.
[10] William Cowper (1849 [1782]). "Conversation." In Grimshawe, Rev. (ed.), *The Works of William Cowper*. London: William Tegg & Co.

9

OVERCOMING ADVERSITY

*Was mich nicht umbringt, macht mich starker.**

—*Friedrich Nietzsche*

There is no education like adversity.

—*Benjamin Disraeli*

Perfeverance [is] more Prevailing than Violence. Many things which cannot be overcome when they are together do yield themfelves up by degrees when they are separated.

—*Plutarch*

THE SUFFERING OF JOB

From the earliest history of humankind, in storytelling, the listeners' attention truly perks up when listening to the stories of how people overcome adversity. To triumph over adversity has always captured human interest. Clearly, these kinds of stories

---

* Translation: That which does not kill me, makes me stronger.

DOI: 10.4324/9781003508939-9

appear to be very much part of the human condition. None of them, however, perhaps captures our imagination more than the story of Job. In all respects, the Book of Job—found in the Ketuvim section of the Hebrew Bible—represents an extremely thoughtful narrative of the complexities of human suffering in the context of strong religious faith. This famous text, believed to have been written between the seventh and fourth centuries BCE, shows how religious faith can sustain a person through any form of adversity. The tale tells how Job maintains his fidelity to God, despite being subjected to the most terrible trials. It makes him a prime example of human suffering. It is hard to imagine a more incredible way of dealing with adversity.

To triumph over adversity has always captured human interest.

Even though all of us have to deal with the trials and tribulations of human life, Job is exceptional due to the sheer number of misfortunes to which he is subjected. In fact, to most of us, the out-and-out comprehensive nature of his suffering would be unimaginable. In that respect, he is a prime example of the observation that bad things can happen to good people. But despite the bad things that he has to endure, he is also an admirable example of how to remain steadfast when everything around you is falling apart. It is no wonder, given the dramatic nature of the story, that being as "patient as Job" has become a universally known expression.

In the Book of Job, he is presented as a saintly man who feared God and always turned away from evil—a man of remarkable moral integrity. Apart from being upright, however, Job also seems to have been a very wealthy person with large landholdings and much livestock. He is also a family man, having seven sons and three daughters. Clearly, with so many blessings, Job seems to be in God's good graces.

But the Book of Job tells us that Satan didn't like Job's good fortune. Troubled by his good life, the angel of darkness vilified Job before the Lord. Initially, God rejected Satan's arguments that Job's piety was merely rooted in his prosperity. Instead, he emphasized again that Job was a perfect and upright man, a person who would always turn away from evil. But when Satan kept on repeating the fact that Job was pious only because he was materially blessed by God, God decided to put Job's faithfulness to the test.

To demonstrate Job's faithfulness, God permitted Satan to take away all of his possessions. Hence, in rapid succession, Job had to deal with one disaster after the other, starting with the death of his children, his servants, and his livestock. And if that by itself wasn't enough, he also had to deal with the destruction of his property. Finally, to cause even more suffering, Job was afflicted with a painful, disfiguring disease. Still, despite all these hardships, Job remained steadfast in his belief in God. He continued to affirm, as he had always done before, the righteousness of God's actions. He would say, "The Lord gave, and the Lord has taken away; may the name of the Lord be praised."[1]

Eventually, after all of Job's suffering—having shown to all and sundry his extreme devotion—God rewarded him. Job's health was restored. He had seven other sons and three daughters, gained back twice as many cattle as he had had before, and lived a long prosperous life, piously and happily.

Of course, what hard times mean to one person can be quite different for another. Many factors will play a role in how you deal with setbacks in your life. Your reactions are very much dependent on your socioeconomic status, cultural context, gender, religious beliefs, and much more. Still, from a storytelling point of view, Job's tale teaches you important lessons about how to deal with suffering and sorrow. Although he was subjected to unfathomable tragedies, he persevered through it all. The main lesson taken from the Book of Job is therefore that people can overcome adversity. Clearly, Job's trials are lessons in steadfastness, patience, and persistence. However, what his narrative also tells you is how adversity can produce endurance, and how endurance may produce character and courage. While being subjected to his various trials, Job had the strength of character to endure all the terrible things happening to him. He would rise above his anger and bitterness. He would not let other people sway him or those who told him that he must have sinned. Instead, as Job's example shows all of us, out of suffering the strongest souls can emerge. Adversity has a way of introducing people to themselves.

Adversity has a way of introducing people to themselves.

Job's cries to God are symbolic of humanity's search for an understanding of human suffering. No wonder that Job's voice, so full of sorrow, desperation, and anger, is a voice that touches all of us. This tragic tale also points out that suffering is an inevitable part of the human condition. With all its sorrow, however, the story of Job is also one of hope. It tells you that adversity can not only make for considerable suffering but also that it can have its positive aspects. People experiencing serious setbacks in life may have a transforming experience; given what they go through, they may look at life in a different way. They may gain a deeper understanding of themselves and their world. The setbacks that they experience may thus help them discover what they are all about. As a matter of fact, adversity can be looked on as an experience during which people become better acquainted with themselves. It may even motivate them to embark on new challenges.

HANDLING ADVERSITY

The Christian apostle Paul wrote that "suffering produces endurance, and endurance produces character, and character produces hope."[2] This suggests that people can attain personal growth through adversity. Although this statement, intuitively at least, seems to make sense, what needs to be added is that traumatic experiences can affect people in many different ways. Clearly, some people will find it extremely difficult to recover from trauma. Thus, despite the value of listening to stories like Job's, the jury is still out about whether personal growth and resilience are the typical outcomes of adversity. Clearly, not everyone has Job's strength of character.

Although adversity can make you stronger, it probably doesn't happen as often as many people like to believe. Adversity may contribute to new insights about life, but the "when" and "how" this happens still aren't very clear. As you may have discovered yourself, not everybody grows from adversity. Even though some people may become stronger, may improve the quality of their relationships, and/or increase their sense of self-esteem, this doesn't happen nearly as often as we would like to believe. For some people, the traumatic experience they have gone through may just be too much. For example, serious setbacks in life like the death of a child or parent, a natural disaster, being physically attacked, experiencing sexual abuse, or being forcibly separated from your family, can cause serious psychological problems. Such traumatic experiences may cause a breaking point in a person's life. Faced with too much adversity, personal growth is most likely out of the question. A more probable outcome will be a deep state of despair. In fact, some effects of tragedy never fully go away.

As far as adverse experiences are concerned, moderation can be a great ally. If the challenges aren't excessive, adversity could contribute to what has been called a post-traumatic growth experience, referring to a positive psychological change that may come to the fore after a life crisis or traumatic event. Such an experience may help you discover what you're really all about. It could provide you with new insights about yourself. In addition, it could contribute to improved relationships with other people. For example, an experience of adversity has been associated with a greater capacity for empathy and compassion.[3] Apparently, if you have gone through challenging experiences, you are more likely to show greater empathy and compassion. You're more likely to support others who are faced with similar stressful situations. Clearly, after what you have personally gone through, you will have greater compassion for yourself as well as for others.

In addition, due to the experience of adversity, it is very likely that you may recognize gratitude in ways that would previously have escaped you, especially in the context of relationships. It appears that once you begin to take note of the things you're grateful for, you begin to lose sight of the things you previously found lacking. And what's more, the experience of gratitude helps you to rethink or reframe what would once have been experienced as stressful. This is one of the benefits of having experienced adversity. Consequently, you may be able to tackle the next challenge with greater confidence. You may be better equipped to take advantage of your mental and physical resources, having become more cognizant of your personal strength. Furthermore, with the conviction that you can manage things better than you did before, due to your newly acquired self-confidence, you may be motivated to pursue new, more challenging goals. All in all, having faced adversity can contribute to an ability to identify new life challenges. It may generate a state of mind that will contribute to an enhanced appreciation of life. It may even further your spiritual growth.

Clearly, narratives about overcoming adversity will always have a very powerful impact. They can serve as an inspiration for your own life. It's what makes these stories so very inspiring. And given the way the story of Job unfolds, it also makes you understand that there can be a silver lining to great tragedy. It points out that good things can emerge from a bad turn of events. It makes you feel better when you think of the challenges that you have in your own life. In more than one way, the story of Job may help you to ward off depressive thoughts and remind you that hardships make you appreciate the good times.

THE RESILIENCE FACTOR

The story of Job tells us that life isn't a rose garden. Nobody escapes pain, fear, and suffering. Yet, as many people like to tell themselves, from pain can come wisdom, from fear can come courage, from suffering can come strength—if you have the virtue of resilience. If the struggle to overcome adversity turns out to be a growth experience, you may feel empowered and triumphant over your struggles. It may even contribute to greater resilience if you are once again faced with challenging situations.

Being resilient means having the mental and physical resources that will help you to overcome future challenges that you may encounter. It is this quality of character that will help you to bounce back from life's challenges and unforeseen difficulties. It may even protect you against emotional and mental disorders. And what the story of Job shows is that not only do you need resilience to make it through hard times, you may also need hard times to build resilience.

From pain can come wisdom, from fear can come courage, from suffering can come strength—if you have the virtue of resilience.

How resilient you will be is very much dictated by a combination of genetics, personal history, environment, and situational factors. Temperamental or personality characteristics that have a genetic base should also be taken into consideration. Most importantly, however, the most significant determinant of how resilient you will be is the quality of your close personal relationships, especially those with your parents and primary caregivers. Clearly, family environments characterized by stability, cohesion, organization, and preservation of routines and rituals are most conducive for strengthening the resilience factor.

Given the importance of resilience, you should ask yourself what you have in your own resilience toolbox. What tools do you have available? Do you have the proper resources to take care of your mental and physical health? Do you know how to take care of yourself when you are stressed? Do you know how to tell a more positive story?

As we learn from the story of Job, resilient people believe in themselves and in their abilities. They have the self-confidence to handle stressful situations and know how to deal with change. They score high on self-efficacy, meaning they believe in their capacity to act in the ways necessary to reach specific goals. Furthermore, resilient people will have an optimistic outlook to life, while remaining realistic. In that respect, resilience can be compared to applied optimism. Generally speaking, such individuals don't dwell on the negative. They look for opportunities that might exist even in the darkest of times. Also, they possess cognitive and emotional flexibility in their thinking. They have excellent problem-solving skills. They have learned to carefully accept what they can't change about a situation and then ask themselves what they can actually change. Their moral compass is strong, they know what they stand for, they have clearly established goals, and work toward them. In that respect, they are action-oriented, not reactive. Furthermore, they are also prepared to reach out to others when they need help. Having realized that they cannot and should not overcome their struggles on their own, they create social networks. Moreover, they recognize how dedication to a worthy cause or a belief in something greater than themselves—religiously or spiritually— will have a resilience-enhancing effect. It gives their life a sense of purpose. It also implies that these people have an altruistic side—they are concerned for others and often possess a degree of selflessness.

Despite these qualities—and taking into consideration that Job was a very special case—it has to be re-emphasized that very high levels of adversity can overtax coping skills and support networks, making for feelings of hopelessness and helplessness. Ultimately, excess adversity may contribute to the feeling of losing control. Such a level of adversity may not be a growth experience. Instead, it may take a toll on your mental health and well-being. In other words, too much hardship can deplete our toolbox of coping skills and put immense pressure on our families, friends, and communities. It may get so bleak that you could fall into a state of depression.

When you long for a life without difficulties, you should remind yourself that oak trees grow strong in contrary winds.

To sum up, even having an enormous capacity for resilience doesn't necessarily mean that horrible experiences will be good for you. Although adversity in some instances can certainly make you stronger, this doesn't mean you should go out of your way looking for bad experiences to toughen you up. That being said, however, difficult life situations often do define what you are all about. In many instances, they can show you what you're made of. Challenging experiences can make you stronger. Consequently, stories of growth stemming from trauma are extremely powerful. Often, they will serve as inspiration for your own lives; Mahatma Gandhi and Nelson Mandela being great examples. Also, what these stories show is that even in our most difficult times—when

Pandora's box has been opened—there can be a little bit of light that will spark the seed of something extremely powerful, something called hope. Furthermore, resilience can help protect you from serious mental health conditions, including depression and anxiety. Clearly, when you become more resilient, it will have a positive effect on your coping skills. It can make you stronger, happier, and more capable of dealing with the challenges that you face in life, work, and in your relationships. When you long for a life without difficulties, you should remind yourself that oak trees grow strong in contrary winds.

Adversity not only builds character but also reveals character.

Therefore, when you tell the story of your life, what will the content be? As the narrator, it will be up to you to decide. What dragons did you have to slay? You must have realized by now that most people didn't have an easy ride to get where they are. You don't develop resilience by going smoothly through life. You develop it by surviving difficult times and challenging adversity. And while on this journey, isn't it also true that adversity not only builds character but also reveals character?

NOTES

[1] Book of Job 1, verses 20–21.
[2] Romans 5, verses 1–5.
[3] Daniel Lim and David DeSteno (2016). "Suffering and Compassion: The Link Among Adverse Life Experiences, Empathy, Compassion and Prosocial Behavior." *Emotion*, 16(2): 175–182.

10

THE INFLUENCERS' WORLD OF MAKE-BELIEVE

Clothes make the man. Naked people have little or no influence on society.
—Mark Twain

A republic may, likewise, be brought back to its original form, without recourse to ordinances for enforcing justice, by the mere virtues of a single citizen, by reason that these virtues are of such influence and authority that good men love to imitate them, and bad men are ashamed to depart from them.
—Niccolò Machiavelli

The tale of adversity in Chapter 9—the dramatic story of Job—brings me to another story, a very contemporary one. It is about Nathalie, a social influencer. Here is her story.

NATHALIE'S TALE OF TALES

Nathalie didn't feel in the greatest shape, yet she wasn't clear what was the matter with her. Whatever it was, she felt quite anxious and had depressive thoughts circling in her mind. She wondered whether it had something to do with her job as an influencer. Although initially rewarding, she now felt it was putting a lot of

DOI: 10.4324/9781003508939-10

pressure on her. An activity that had once seemed like a lot of fun was fast losing its glamor.

Nathalie made a living by using her personal profile to promote products for fashion brands on social media via beautiful photos, video clips, and text messages. Initially, she had been quite excited about what she was doing. Not only did this kind of work give her an excellent opportunity to express herself but she also valued the independence that it provided. Although as an influencer Nathalie wasn't one of the mega-celebrities, like film stars with millions of followers, she still had a substantial number of people visiting her platform. Above all, she liked telling stories on her digital stage.

However, after the initial satisfaction, Nathalie had come to realize that it could be quite mentally taxing to derive a reliable income from promotions on various social media outlets. As things stood, she felt tied to a static, somewhat inauthentic identity—a false self. She was constantly torn between the need to produce beautiful feeds and the desire to be truly herself. A factor that further depleted her state of mind was the constant pressure she experienced in having to interact with her audience at all hours with very little or no slack time. Storytelling could become exhausting. Adding to these feelings of aggravation was having to deal with people who strongly disagreed with what she had to say and whose reactions regularly amounted to cyberbullying.

So, despite her success as an influencer/storyteller, there were times when Nathalie wondered why her followers were at all inclined to buy the products that she was recommending. What was so special about what she was doing? In fact, what was influence marketing all about? Was the way she tried to influence people through social media, the manner in which she told stories, different from the ways it had been done in the past?

Nathalie remembered reading the bestseller *The Hidden Persuaders* by Vance Packard, which revealed how advertisers used subtle psychological methods to tap into people's unconscious desires in order to persuade them to buy certain products.[1] At the time she thought that the way these advertisers tried to condition the reflexes of consumers at a semi-conscious level was rather disturbing. Yet, was she, without full awareness, now doing something very similar?

What Nathalie did realize, however, was that people had become tired of traditional forms of advertising. She knew that consumers (especially millennials) had become cynical about the many promises made by companies advertising their brands. Clearly, trying to convince people to buy goods through conventional advertising channels such as radio, billboards, or television commercials was not as powerful as it used to be. Instead, people were spending an increasing amount of time on digital channels. Also, Nathalie wondered to what degree people still trusted the more traditional celebrity endorsements. It made her reappraise the effectiveness of such advertising campaigns and question whether they made a real impact. Nathalie also understood that many businesses had also concluded that the more traditional advertising methods were too expensive.

In this respect, influencers were much more affordable. Many businesses had come to believe that using influencers was considerably more effective in conveying the core message of their brand, driving sales through greater brand awareness. Of course, she knew that in the influencing world there were different scales of influencers. There were smaller influencers and minor celebrities, and then there were influencers like the Kardashians who were considered to be among the most influential celebrities worldwide. Whatever stories they told, millions of people were listening to them.

Nathalie recognized that the main difference between celebrity endorsements (often used for more conventional marketing) and social media content creators was that of social distance. She knew that as a social media creator she came across as more genuine and trustworthy, and it seemed that this was what consumers were really craving in a saturated advertising market. Clearly, social media platforms run by influencers were a means of encouraging greater customer engagement.

In parallel with the way technology had transformed the way people were interacting with each other, a platform like hers had changed the way potential consumers were accessing content. In fact, her promotions could be seen as a form of word-of-mouth on a grand scale. In her efforts to get close to her audience, Nathalie knew that she had become a role model for many of her followers. However, while she was promoting a particular lifestyle, she was also endorsing various brands and products. Still, the question remained, what subtle psychological forces were at work that made her influencing activities so effective? She decided to list some of the variables that were factors of her success.

Expert power

For a start, Nathalie realized that to reach an audience, and be a successful influencer, people who visited her platform needed to recognize that she had real knowledge and *expertise* about the topics that she was addressing. Only when people accepted her expertise about these matters could she make a real impact. Therefore, a sine qua non for being an effective influencer was to prove her credibility. Like experts in other fields, she had to appear authoritative about the matters she talked about in order for followers to go along with her suggestions. In fact, people seem to be hardwired to follow people they view as authority figures—people whom they believe possess accurate information. In her case, having spent considerable time developing an expertise in fashion, Nathalie knew that she had built a solid reputation.

Pseudo-intimacy

Nathalie appreciated, however, that expertise alone wouldn't be good enough and that it was just as important to build meaningful connections with her audience. She needed to imbue them with feelings of what can best be described as *pseudo-intimacy*. To achieve this, she used every aspect of her personality to connect directly with her followers: looking right into the camera to make virtual eye contact, trying to tell compelling stories while doing her pitches, and responding rapidly to their "likes" and comments during live events. And such attentiveness paid off, as her followers responded instinctively to these physical signals of social connection, making them feel close to her. Consequently, in contrast to the traditional promotional activities of celebrities, the connection with her followers seemed to be at a much more personal level. Simply by the way she related to them, she had become the celebrity next door. Compared with the glamorous celebrity endorsements, Nathalie appeared more down to earth, relatable, and approachable.

The way Nathalie was presenting herself made her followers actively follow her day-to-day activities, wanting to be like her. It seemed as if, for them, there was always that imaginary possibility of getting in touch with her. By sharing personal photos and videos while telling her stories, her followers felt a sense of connection and intimacy, as though they could get to know her in real life. In fact, her life choices, fashion statements, lifestyle, and way of living had become the dream of many of them.

The advantage of this seemingly personal, emotional connection, where she was willing to share life experiences and often private moments, was that her followers trusted her like they would trust real friends. And, with this perceived lack of distance, her followers engaged more with the brands or products she was endorsing.

Trust through repeated exposure

Nathalie also came to understand that, to her followers, the *frequent exposure* of her communications added to this trust equation and that, generally speaking, people prefer to deal with those who are familiar to them. As time went by—given all the pictures, videos, and live streams she was sharing—she had become a consistent presence in her followers' lives. She grasped that from a psychological perspective the frequency of exposure directly affected their allegiance to her. The more she exposed her followers to specific content, the more they would accept the content that she was presenting. Subsequently, her followers would assimilate her view about various matters in their own beliefs and preferences. This made it more likely that they would make purchasing decisions based on the advice she gave and the products she endorsed.

Overcoming information overload

Nathalie appreciated that a further factor strengthened her role as an influencer: in general, making a sound decision about buying a specific product requires thorough research and knowledge, something that easily left people suffering from *information overload*. Many found it increasingly difficult to sort through all the information needed to make a truly informed decision, and one way to avoid this was to follow the suggestions of somebody else. Taking this process into consideration, Nathalie realized that she might serve as some kind of filter, using her perceived authority, expertise, and trustworthiness to provide focus to the information that was needed. As a filter, her display of knowledge gave a certain credibility to her advice and helped her followers by shaping their decisions.

The sheeple effect

Almost all human beings are hardwired to behave like *sheeples*— prone to responding innately to ingrained social patterns—and Nathalie was aware of this.[2] Similar to the herding behavior found among animals, she saw how large numbers of people would act in the same fashion as a result of being programmed to connect deeply with people who behave similarly. Influencer marketing seemed to play directly into humanity's natural desire for belonging, to be part of a group. Given these psychological behavior patterns, Nathalie saw that the successful influencer was one who took advantage of this innate herd mentality to fit in, and that followers were inclined to do what she or he did or said. As herd animals, many of her followers held the belief that popular things must also be good things; that is, they felt more secure in making choices that appeared to be popular with other people. An influencer with a sizeable audience seemed to verify their trustworthy expertise, simply because so many others approved of what he or she was doing. Consequently, Nathalie discovered that the more followers she had, the more credible she appeared. In addition, some people were concerned that if they didn't join this bandwagon and make similar choices to the rest of the followers, they could end up losing out—yet another reason to copy the actions of others.

The illusion of control

Another factor that played a role in Nathalie's effectiveness as an influencer can be best described as the *illusion of control*. Compared with the more subtle influence exerted through advertisements, in the case of influencers people are able to choose certain content by following or subscribing to those in whom they are interested. And, although perhaps more subtle in some respects, traditional forms of advertising that appear across favorite websites and social networks are frequently considered irritating or even intrusive. More frustrating still is the regularity of these ads, their placement on webpages, and their frequent lack of relevance or bad targeting, all of which can lead to a sense of powerlessness. In contrast, influencer promotions are not imposed on consumers, but are selected by them. This plays into another basic human characteristic: human beings prefer not to be in the position of passive recipient and naturally desire some base level of power and control for the purpose of survival. By using the services of an influencer such as Nathalie, people no longer saw themselves as passive consumers of advertising. On the contrary, they had a greater feeling of control, as not only were they choosing *whom* they followed but also the *content* of their choice.

Human beings prefer not to be in the position of passive recipient and naturally desire some base level of power and control for the purpose of survival.

The reciprocity factor

Nathalie was also familiar with what could be called the *reciprocity factor*, which seemed to be an important psychological component of influencer marketing. From what she understood, this reciprocity factor worked as follows: when people receive something of value, they are much more likely to return this favor by giving something back. Nathalie realized that this principle also applied to the efforts she made to influence her followers. When her followers perceived themselves to have a personal connection with her, they appeared to be more willing—obliged even—to provide her with help and assistance in return. And what better way to do so than to buy the products she was endorsing?

When people receive something of value, they are much more likely to return this favor by giving something back.

The attractiveness bias

What had also come to Nathalie's attention in the context of her role was the *attractiveness bias*. This cognitive bias seems to be an inherent social pattern, determining anything from who will become famous to who will get hired. Apparently, human beings tend to be more trusting of people who are good looking, perceiving them to be more intelligent, competent, and sociable in comparison with less attractive people. And bearing in mind the theme of this book, in storytelling the "evil" characters in traditional fairytales are more often portrayed as "ugly," as if their appearance reflects their underlying character.

Since the attractiveness bias seems to be hardwired into society as a whole, as well as in the individual, marketeers can naturally capitalize on it through influencer marketing. Given the effect of this bias, certain influencers are more effective than others. In fact, the attractiveness bias could even reinforce people's ideas about the authority and expertise of the people they follow. For example, coming across as attractive may lead to a greater sense of trust that could in turn rub off on brands or products that the influencer is endorsing. It appears that when an attractive person works with a particular brand, it creates the association that the brand is also attractive.

The "evil" characters in traditional fairytales are often portrayed as "ugly," as if their appearance reflects their underlying character.

The halo effect

To add to the various psychological dynamics of influencing, Nathalie also knew that there was something that could best be described as the *halo effect*—that is, positive feelings toward a person, brand, or product in one area could positively influence people's feelings about them in another area. Hence, when a person is perceived as being an expert in one domain, this expertise easily becomes transferable to another. Consequently, Nathalie had discovered that, while telling her stories, she could carry over her authority in one area of expertise to another. Undeniably, she had been taking advantage of this psychological process. Based purely on the pre-existing trust they had developed, people would follow her advice on matters on which she had no expertise.

THE INFLUENCERS' DILEMMA

Although the long-term effects of social media use among people who create content and those who consume it are still unknown, what is recognized is that living too much of your life online can have negative mental health implications.[3] Excessive use of social media appears to be associated with anxiety, depression, and even physical ailments. The irony is that social media technology, principally designed to bring people together, can just as easily make them feel even lonelier and more isolated. This raises the question as to how far its advantages, such as connecting with friends and family or finding information, outweigh potentially harmful elements, including cyberbullying, rumor mongering, and exposure to the unrealistic views of other people's lives. In fact, any astute examination of the many psychological processes at play may conclude that a constant search for recognition and attention by way of social media can become a toxic force with detrimental effects; it has the power to leave you feeling hurt or needing more attention. What adds to its potentially negative impact is that the algorithms behind social media favor the sensational, most shocking, and often most damaging news. All too often, these platforms spread misinformation, encouraging their users to engage with fake news more than with fact-checked news.

Despite these proven negative implications of significant social media use, most people will be reluctant to let go. Clearly, many of these platforms activate the brain's reward center by releasing dopamine, a feel-good chemical linked to pleasurable activities such as sex, food, and social interaction. In reality, many social media platforms are specifically designed to be addictive and, without consistent exposure to these stimuli, people may experience withdrawal symptoms. It is no wonder that high use of social media increases the likelihood of people feeling anxious, depressed, or lonely; it has even been shown to increase the risk of self-harm and suicide.[4] With some understanding of these addictive patterns, both influencers and followers should be aware of these risk factors.

The influencers

Nathalie initially liked being an influencer. What she didn't realize, however, was the responsibility or pressure that came with it. She was unprepared for the fact that having her whole life invested in telling stories on social media could have a serious downside. As time went by, she discovered that her online world was becoming increasingly overwhelming and exhausting. Constantly having to churn out fresh digital material for mass consumption—often by sharing intimate details of her life—came with real psychological wear and tear. As she had said before, telling stories can be exhausting.

Telling stories can be exhausting.

Once she had accumulated a large following on her platform, Nathalie began to feel constrained by the types of posts she should create. She felt she could no longer be her true self, and instead had to portray a version of her life that became increasingly inauthentic; in short, she felt she was presenting a false self. Adding to her sense of discomfort was the feeling of being invaded.

The degree to which people were constantly analyzing everything she said and posted could feel quite intrusive. Additionally, comparing herself to other high-status influencers—making upward social comparisons—added to the stress equation.

While occupational stress certainly isn't unique, the kind of interactions Nathalie was dealing with as an influencer could be quite hostile. Given the stories she told, she was also regularly exposed to violent threats and verbal cruelty from some of her followers—reactions that had a detrimental effect on her sense of self-worth. It was very difficult not to take these comments personally and, as time passed, she noticed that they were taking a toll on her mental health, especially when she had been exposed to online abuse. Nathalie felt that this seemed somewhat ironic, considering she was attempting to promote a healthy lifestyle to her followers. It made her realize that influencing by itself wasn't necessarily a mental health-promoting activity.

In addition, Nathalie noted that being an influencer had an addictive quality. Neurologically, interacting with her followers on her platform supplied intermittent yet constant hits of dopamine. Could it be that, if she wasn't using social media outlets, she would be subject to feelings of dopamine withdrawal? Might this put her at an even higher risk of anxiety and depression compared with people who didn't make a living on the Internet? Furthermore, she wondered what kind of effect it would it have on her when money and fame were thrown into the mix.

The followers

For social media followers, platforms with a strong focus on social comparison may have the most detrimental effects, causing reduced satisfaction with appearance, low self-evaluations, negative mood states, feelings of insecurity, and general feelings of anxiety. Images and the stories told online can often be harmful to people's self-confidence as they fail to represent the average human being's body or life. People are constantly comparing themselves on the basis of such images and stories, trying to figure out if they are more or less attractive, smart, or accomplished than other people. Instagram—more than any other platform—can confuse people's endeavors at social comparison. With Instagram, they have immediate access to idealized images that fail to give an accurate representation of what the world is really like.[5] After all, people tend to post only their best images on Instagram, using filters that make them look as perfect as possible. When looking at these beautiful images, it is easy to forget that Instagram does *not* represent reality; that is, people can get a false sense of what the average person looks like and, consequently, feel worse about themselves.

INFLUENCING: A ROLLER COASTER RIDE

Influencing has become a popular and, for some, lucrative activity. Clearly, the stories these people tell have a role to play in contemporary society. However, as I have discussed in this chapter, constant social media also has its drawbacks both for influencers and for those who access its content. In fact, the dissonance between social media portrayals and reality can be unsettling, and remaining mindful that social media isn't "real life" is easier said than done. Influencing in itself isn't *all* bad—it can certainly be used for the good, with followers finding connection, inspiration, and ideas when they tune into their favorites. However, the negative mental health effects from using this medium remain. The pressures put on influencers can lead them to mask issues such as serious health concerns, even as they continue to promote lifestyles that aren't sustainable for anyone. In such cases both influencers and followers bear the consequences.

The dissonance between social media portrayals and reality can be unsettling, and remaining mindful that social media isn't "real life" is easier said than done.

Understanding, or at least being aware of, these potentially toxic dynamics is something from which both influencers and followers can benefit. They should recognize the psychological and physiological implications of influencing and become more mindful about the way they tell their stories—that is, the way information is presented and consumed online. And they better realize that it is rare that the content they view and the individuals they follow, however persuasive, portray a life that does not encompass some degree of "make-believe."

It has been suggested that one way to continue this process of make-believe, without the stress that comes with it, is to create virtual humans. Presently, such a transformation is happening in South Korea, where computer-generated influencers have become quite popular. Created with 3D modeling technology and artificial intelligence (AI), these avatars seem to be an attractive, and much cheaper, substitute.[6] They are even able to interact with their audience. And as opposed to real-life influencers, their background stories are massaged in such a way to make it is less likely that the companies they represent have to worry about possible reputational damage, as has been the case with several of their human counterparts. However, there is currently no evidence as to whether the stories these avatars tell have the same emotional influence on their audience as those of real people.

With respect to real-life influencers and their followers, they would do well to monitor carefully their mental health when they interact. There can be too much of what isn't really a good thing. Looking after their mental health is an essential part of their overall health. After all, all of us, at some point in our lives, will have mental health issues. Anyone can be affected. Self-care isn't a luxury and suffering in silence isn't good for anyone.

All of us, at some point in our lives, will have mental health issues.

NOTES

[1] Vance Packard (1957). *The Hidden Persuaders*. New York: David McKay Company.
[2] Manfred F. R. Kets de Vries (2024). *The Darker Side of Leadership: Pythons Devouring Crocodiles*. New York: Routledge.
[3] Melissa G. Hunt, Rachel Marx, Courtney Lipson, and Jordyn Young (2018). "No More FOMO: Limiting Social Media Decreases Loneliness and Depression." *Journal of Social and Clinical Psychology*, 37(10): 751–768; Ujala Zubair, Muhammad K. Khan, and Muna Albashari (2023). "Link Between Excessive Social Media Use and Psychiatric Disorders." *Annals of Medicine & Surgery*, 85(4): 875–878.

4 Zubair et al. ibid.

5 Kim Elsesser (2021). "Here's How Instagram Harms Young Women According to Research." *Forbes*, 5 October.

6 Jessie Jeung and Gawon Bae (2022). "Forever Young, Beautiful and Scandal-free: The Rise of South Korea's Virtual Influencers." *CNN*, 16 August.

11

SLEEPING YOUR WAY TO THE TOP

It is heavenly, when I overcome
My earthly desires
But nevertheless, when I'm not successful,
It can also be quite pleasurable.

—Leo Tolstoy

The behavior of a human being in sexual matters is often a prototype for
the whole of his other modes of reaction in life.

—Sigmund Freud

But that is how men are! Ungrateful and never satisfied. When you don't
have them they hate you because you won't; and when you do have them
they hate you again, for some other reason.

—D. H. Lawrence

You may well be confused on reading this chapter title—but here I'm using it not to recommend either the effect of a good night's sleep on work performance, or taking the route that the usual understanding of the phrase implies. However, I am going to look at the way some people use their sex appeal and sexual prowess to further their career. There are many different ways to reach the summit of an organization, some more creative than others.

DOI: 10.4324/9781003508939-11

Of course, the traditional road to the top is demonstrating that you have a good story to tell and that you are a competent corporate citizen. Some people, however, conclude that they aren't going to make it through competence alone. Consequently, they decide to add an extra dimension to the mix, the "extra" in their story being their sex appeal. *Homo sapiens* is a sexual being, and they recognize that whatever the circumstances sex does matter. And although, personally, you may object to using sex as a way to the top, you may also have discovered that for others this can be a highly effective way to clear the road to success.

THE SEXUAL EXCHANGE

Unquestionably, there are many instances when sexuality has nothing to do with a person's career progression. Sexual exchange is not a *sine qua non* to reach top management positions. But, in truth, sex is of greater importance in organizational life than many people are willing to admit. Given *Homo sapiens'* makeup, sexuality is ever present and, if it is acted upon, a person's sex appeal can be used in many different ways.

Take, for example, Pamela Harriman, the British-born US Ambassador to France from 1993 to 1997. Baron Elie de Rothschild called her a "European Geisha," while others described her as the "last courtesan."[1] And as a *femme fatale*, she seemed to have been one of a kind. From what we can infer about her life, Mrs. Harriman knew, very much like Scheherazade, not only how to make men feel important but also how to take advantage of their weaknesses. Given the time she lived in, however, she may not have had much of a choice if she wanted to be successful. As she said herself, describing her traditional upper-class British background, "I was born in a world where a woman was totally controlled by men. The boys were allowed to go off to school. The girls were kept home, educated by governesses. That was the way things were."[2] Given the environment she grew up in, she must have decided that the only way for a woman to gain power and succeed in life was by captivating and influencing men with real power. The tales of her many escapades, seducing some of the world's richest and most attractive men, were the stuff of legend. During her lifetime, she married three powerful men and left many angry women behind. One of her more noteworthy comments was, "I'd rather have bad things written about me than to be forgotten."[3] Everything being equal, using sex as a weapon became Mrs. Harriman's rather pragmatic way to rise to the top.

Does Mrs. Harriman's story sound familiar? Even if not acted out openly, using sex as a weapon is quite a familiar pattern in organizational life. Take for example the entertainment industry, where the notion of having to deal with the "casting couch" is notorious. However, as Mrs. Harriman's example illustrates, engaging in sex for ulterior motives is an activity that is found in the worlds of politics, finance, publishing, media, and many others.

Although the practice may be frowned upon, the hard reality is that sex can be the key to the fast track and can be used in many ways. Specific tactics vary from simply making a good impression, based on good looks and charm, to telling seductive stories to entice someone to a quick fling in return for favors, to forging a long-lasting relationship with a person in power. Seduction doesn't necessarily need to involve actually having an affair. Sex can also happen accidentally, with no ulterior motive on either person's part. Sometimes, despite all appearances, there are situations when sex has *nothing* to do with a person's rise to power. For whatever reason, it could very well be that a powerful individual has decided to further the career of a specific person. But given the way *Homo sapiens* is programmed, the sexual fantasy that there is more than meets the eye will never be far away.

Given the ubiquitousness of sexual fantasies, people often assume that when a woman reaches a powerful position, her success must be the result of sleeping her way to the top, using her femininity and sexuality to reach the circles of power; otherwise, how could she be where she is now? Sadly, far too many successful women are familiar with such an accusation, having heard it said about other women as well as themselves. And such accusations often turn out to be entirely false. There may, of course, be situations where an accusation is based on a misplaced inference about a sexual relationship that was consensual and completely unrelated to a woman's career progress. And we must not forget, on the seedier side, brought recently to the fore with behavior of the film producer Harvey Weinstein and his tawdry "casting couch," that there have been many incidences whereby women were forced into sex by men in power.

Yet, the question remains, why are women so readily reproached? Why are they so quickly accused of having slept their way to the top and using sexual favors to obtain their position? It could be that such rumor mongering is a malicious, spiteful tactic employed by their organizational rivals who envy their success and want to tarnish their reputation. Such people dismiss the accomplishments of these women. Very often, however, the success of these women had nothing to do with sex and is all about ability.

But, looking at it another way, what is so bad about sleeping your way to the top? In organizational life, if you are ambitious, isn't it reasonable to use all the tools available to you? Isn't that part of life's reality? Even if some people do sleep their way to the top, it does not mean that they're untalented or unfit for the position. As the example of Mrs. Harriman illustrates, they might see it as the only way to overcome serious hindrances in their career or society in general.

In fact, despite our ambivalence about using sex as an instrument for career success, taking a hard look at organizational life, it is self-evident that a substantial number of executives are quite prepared to trade sex for promotion. And I'm not just referring to women here. Both men and women seem inclined to do so. Sex and power have always had an intimate connection. Remember Henry Kissinger's assertion that "Power is the greatest aphrodisiac"?[4] Actually, whether power begets sex or sex begets power, the distinction may be hard to discern. What is clear, however, is that there seems to be a positive correlation between the two. Taking advantage of your sex appeal is part of life, the business world being no exception. Therefore, if you have the opportunity to get where you want to be by having sex, why not take advantage of it? Why shouldn't women use their "erotic capital"—beauty, sex appeal, charm, and dress code—to get ahead at the place they work? And why can't men do the same?

Sex and power have always had an intimate connection.

For example, take the story of Tom, a middle manager in a family-controlled business in the specialized machinery industry, a person with great ambitions but whose prospects didn't seem to be very promising. The competition for the top positions in the company was intense. Fortunately, Tom got a lucky break. At the company's Christmas party, he met a woman who turned out to be the oldest daughter of the CEO, who was also a major shareholder in the firm. Even though Tom wasn't physically attracted to her, he was attracted to the possibility that she represented a potential road to the top for him. He recognized that by using his sex appeal, he could advance his career. Starting with the party, Tom dazzled the CEO's daughter with his charms; they began to date, and soon married. Subsequently, his newly minted father-in-law recommended him for a top management program at a premier business school. The idea behind this recommendation was to prepare him for a newly created senior position in the organization.

So, it isn't just women who use sex as a way to get to the top. Men do the same. However, people are less disturbed when men use sex to rise to the top than when women do. Clearly, people are much more forgiving when a man uses his sexual capital and may even congratulate him for his smart career move. Unfortunately, they are unlikely to do so for a woman.

But why is this the case? Do men use sex more subtly, making it more difficult to spot what they're doing? Do they have a better story to tell? Do they weave sexual innuendo into their charisma, confidence, and assertiveness? Or has it something to do with people's misogynistic attitudes? Could it actually be that many men are seriously prejudiced against women? That some have a deep-seated fear of the "feminine"?

Elaborating on this point, if you pay attention to more unconscious thought processes, it could very well be that many men fear being dominated, controlled, or abandoned by women. Often, a man's apparent self-sufficiency is nothing more than a façade that is put up to hide such fears. Consequently, given the psychological fragility of such men, successful women are quickly perceived as a threat. These women reawaken early childhood apprehensions of how they were treated by female caretakers. They remember how they feared being dominated, controlled, or even abandoned by women (having them withdraw their affection) in the past. After all, they were once dependent on a mother's love for survival. These psychological dynamics, centered around highly ambivalent feelings, could be a possible explanatory factor as to why some men are so quick to accuse women of using sex as a weapon when, ironically, they themselves seem to get off scot-free if they do the same.

As the example of Tom illustrates, men are no strangers to the idea of using sex as a weapon and many of them, when they realize that it can be to their advantage, will not hesitate to use it. We saw how Tom went to great lengths to get closer to his boss's daughter, and other men will not think twice of befriending their female bosses to move up the career ladder. Some men are even alert to singling out gay senior executives with the aim of taking advantage of them.

A THICK SKIN IS A GIFT

However, if you're thinking of using sex as a means of career advancement, perhaps you'd better think twice. If you decide to sleep your way to the top, you need to have a thick skin. You should expect a barrage of criticism and disdain when people hear your life story, for, even though these activities are a reality, many people consider such a life strategy unfair. They view the resulting career advancement as undeserved. In other words, they may tell stories about you, and insinuate that you lack the talent or experience necessary for the position that you have obtained. And, as you may have inferred, if you are a woman, some accusers may even go into misogynistic overdrive, using it as "proof" that women are so incompetent that sex is the only way for them to advance in life. Others may label you extremely calculating. They may even call you a slut. In that respect, as a woman, you're getting a rotten deal compared with men who do the same. As is clear for all to see, for men this career strategy is considered more acceptable; some male colleagues in the company may even label you a real man for being able to conquer women senior to you.

If you decide to sleep your way to the top, you need to have a thick skin.

In conclusion, what becomes clear listening to these stories is that sexuality can be a powerful and potent tool for everyone in the workplace. But although sexuality will be an ever-present force, you should also realize that if you decide to use it, most likely, it will tarnish your reputation. Thus, the message is obvious. Both men and women with an overactive libido should be careful. If you have a powerful sex drive, you may all too quickly be tripped up by the very "force" needed to help you achieve what's truly important to you. In fact, notwithstanding the centrality of sexuality in human existence, sex and emotional manipulation are dangerous companions. Relying on sex appeal—that is, becoming too dependent on your sexual prowess instead of talent—can a very risky strategy. Much can be said about the force of sublimation—transference of the more unacceptable impulses into social actions, or behavior, that are less damaging and more productive. Thus, it may be much wiser to rechannel your lustful feelings and shift your sexual energy from the physical to the psychic plane—especially if you're interested in living a more peaceful and purposeful life. Too much excitement doesn't necessarily bring happiness. Too much excitement doesn't necessarily make for a satisfied life. Of course, it doesn't mean that you should avoid life. Life isn't an afterthought. It is not a rehearsal.

NOTES

1 Stuart Husband (January 2024). "Pamela Harriman: Of Vice and Men." *The Rake*, https://therake.com/stories/pamela-harriman-of-vice-and-men
2 *Newsweek* (6 February 1997). "A Woman of Means," https://www.newsweek.com/woman-means-175062

[3] Ibid.

[4] *The New York Times* (19 January 1971). See Michael C. Thomsett and Jean Freestone Thomsett (2008). *War and Conflict Quotations: A Worldwide Dictionary of Pronouncements from Military Leaders, Politicians, Philosophers, Writers and Others.* Jefferson, NC & London: McFarland.

12

I WANT TO HAVE A LIFE

There is no such thing on earth as an uninteresting subject; the only thing that can exist is an uninterested person.

—G. K. Chesterton

The art of life is more like the wrestler's art than the dancer's.

—Marcus Aurelius

If you cut up a large diamond into little bits, it will entirely lose the value it had as a whole; and an army divided up into small bodies of soldiers, loses all its strength. So a great intellect sinks to the level of an ordinary one, as soon as it is interrupted and disturbed, its attention distracted and drawn off from the matter in hand; for its superiority depends upon its power of concentration—of bringing all its strength to bear upon one theme.

—Arthur Schopenhauer

Here's another story. Philip's tale of woe sounded like a luxury problem. For outsiders, it looked as if he had a very successful life. As CEO of a large, highly profitable firm that continued to grow at a steady rate, he had all the appearances of having a stellar career. Philip should have been quite content. But he wasn't. According to his own story, as he told it, he felt like a hamster on

DOI: 10.4324/9781003508939-12

a treadmill, running aimlessly at an increasingly faster pace. He felt he had no life. Although there had been good moments in the past, they were now much rarer. Presently, he was dissatisfied and felt little pleasure. It was the reason he said, "I want to have a life!"

So how can we unpack the root of Philip's discontent? There were elements of truth in what he was saying. He described his life as a series of never-ending assignments. Other images include a straitjacket from which he couldn't escape. He also felt like he was living other people's lives. There were too many "oughts" and "shoulds" to be taken care of. Often, it seemed as if other people's needs were drowning out his own. Instead of doing things he wanted to do, he experienced his activities as meaningless.

Philip's personal life was a mess. His wife, complaining he was never present, physically or mentally, had left him and he was living alone. His children had left home and had very little to do with him. They were living their own lives. And even though he had the occasional girlfriend, none of them turned into a meaningful relationship. Most of them he would describe as gold diggers.

As things currently stood, Philip didn't feel very well, mentally or physically. Even though he had hired a personal trainer to help him to take care of his body, he rarely used her services. In fact, he missed most appointments. In addition, he had poor sleeping habits and suffered from a serious case of insomnia, worrying about all the things that needed to be done. Not surprisingly, sleep deprivation made him feel very tired—a factor that affected his decision-making capabilities.

All in all, although Philip's outward life looked like a success, his inner life was in total disarray. He was experiencing a complete sense of futility about his life. It felt like he was sleepwalking through it, without meaning or consciousness.

AUTHORING A FULFILLING LIFE

What's been happening to Philip could also happen to you. There might come a point in your life when you are tired of the way you've been living it. And as you may feel increasingly distraught about what's happening to you, this can present an opportunity to make positive life changes. You may even fantasize about making a complete overhaul of your life. Of course, a more realistic scenario would be to start with a number of subtle changes that move you in the direction of the life you would like to live. And while there's no such thing as having a perfect life, in small ways you could begin to have a better life. After all, you should be the author of your own destiny.

There might come a point in your life when you are tired of the way you've been living it.

The question becomes, what steps can you take to live your life to the fullest? How can you live your own life, not the one other people expect of you? And how can you live more authentically? Eventually, when you look back at your life, wouldn't you like to say: it was a great life and I lived it to the fullest? In other words, how will you be able to tell a more positive story about yourself?

To give this life a start, an effective way to begin is to envision your life as you would like it to be in the future. You should see this as the first step to take to get things moving in that direction. And a major part of this envisioning process is to imagine the activities that give you energy, that make you feel good and happy. Of course, you should keep in mind that happiness is not a goal in itself. It is a by-product of a life well lived. Still, if you want to live your best life, an important part is to design happy moments for yourself and create memories that have a lasting impact.

But while you're trying to do so, also keep in mind that changing behavior patterns isn't easy. Trying to change the way you live will take much effort and persistence and can be quite uncomfortable. Often, it can cause pangs of anxiety. And these feelings of anxiety need to be dealt with. If not, they will prevent you from creating your best life.

A common reason why you may feel anxious when making changes to your life is that you may have tried making changes before that ended in failure. Given the disappointment, you may be reluctant to try again. Also, though you feel stuck you may not actually know what is holding you back. That said, you may not realize that these feelings of anxiety are the cause of your reluctance to make any changes to your life. Consequently, these forces inside you need attention.

To begin, you will need to take a journey into your inner world and figure out what's blocking you and holding you back. If, however, you already recognize that your past is influencing your present behavior, you can start to make a conscious effort to deal with the ways you want to change. You should try to tell yourself a more hopeful story.

In many of my conversations with senior leaders, the full life that they seek stems from the common desire to fulfill the truest expression of themselves—meaning they want to become the best that they can be. As humans, we seek to learn, grow, and evolve as well as take pleasure out of life. The only way to do so, however, is by having new experiences that push us beyond our current capabilities, beliefs, and boundaries. But if you want to take this route, you need to be proactive and take control over your life. You need to focus on the things that you *can* change. And you need to focus on the things that you *can* act upon.

THE JOURNEY TO A LIFE WELL LIVED

So, how do you begin? For a starter question—one that has been addressed in previous chapters—you should ask yourself: *Who am I? What am I all about? Who would I like to be?* And if you're able to visualize this person, try to be this person. And in this context, ask yourself: *What do I love to do?* Then, try to do the things you love to do. In addition, ask yourself: *Who do I love?* Then, make an effort to love these people.

The secret of learning to live a fulfilled life is to realize that every-thing you do in the outer world begins in your inner world.

Finally, ask yourself: *What are my hopes for the future?* Then, make an effort to pursue these hopes. Here are some specific steps that you can take:

1   *Know what it means to be you.* To start with, the secret of learn-ing to live a fulfilled life is to realize that everything you do in the outer world begins in your inner world. If you want to

have the life you love living, you must first know what such a life means to you. This implies knowing what it means to *be you*. To be who you are, and to become what you are capable of becoming, should be your purpose in life. You shouldn't be defined by someone else's standards or definition of success. Consequently, if you want to live authentically, you need to figure out who you really are by understanding your drivers, what you're deeply passionate about and what makes you feel most alive. This implies increasing your level of self-consciousness to identify the things that are purposeful and meaningful in your inner life in order to make wise choices in your outer life. It also means that you should pay attention to your shadow side. You should recognize that what this shadow side represents will be an important part of you. It is not something that you should suppress. It *has* to be acknowledged. You need to realize that inclusiveness will make for greater authenticity.

To be who you are, and to become what you are capable of becoming, should be your purpose in life.

---

2   *Let go of unpleasant past experiences.* Then, you should also take the time to "sculpt" your inner world. Often, the only real obstacle in your path to a fulfilling life is you and your past. Hence, you need to work through all the hurts, heartbreaks, and disappointments that you have experienced, practicing self-compassion to let go of these unhappy past experiences. In fact, freedom is what you do with what has been done to you. Thus, an important part of living life to the fullest is the ability to let go of the unpleasant experiences from the past that are affecting your present behavior. Knowing the origins of the things that hold you back will enable you to make a conscious effort to act differently in the future. It will help you to move forward.

3   *Practice empathy and compassion.* While you're on this inner journey, you would do well to practice being empathic and compassionate. Having empathy will enable you to get out

of your insular narcissistic bubble and, despite the fact that everyone is different, appreciate life from another person's point of view. The same can be said about compassion, which will enable you to reach out to people. Being empathic and compassionate means recognizing that the same humanity, desire for meaning, fulfillment and security exist in everyone, even if expressed uniquely. In this context, one simple way of expressing empathy and compassion is to try to do a kind deed every day. After all, kindness begets kindness and there is no better way to grow than to help others to grow.

Freedom is what you do with what has been done to you.

---

4 *Exercise self-care.* There is also the question of self-care. Your body is the place where you live and if your body is falling apart, if you're unhealthy or struggling with illness, it will be difficult to live life fully. Self-care is integrative and also involves taking care of yourself mentally, emotionally, physically, and spiritually. Unfortunately, too many people focus on one area and forget the others. When you're able to take good care of yourself, it is going to be much easier to support and care for others.

5 *Discover your calling.* As so many of us spend most of our time at work, a key challenge for a fulfilling life will be to find a job that best fits who you are. An important part of living your best life is to discover your calling—that special work or consuming occupation that you feel passionate about. To get there, however, you need to ask yourself what makes you feel good and fully alive. If you feel bored, unfulfilled, and unhappy when you're at work, it's a cue to take a look at what you're doing and whether you need to make changes. Before doing so, you should keep in mind that the activities that you like are related to your inner world. If you don't experience pleasure in your work, you need to find out why and what's holding you back. Could it be old habits, limiting beliefs, or the stories that you're

telling yourself? If you have a better understanding of what you're all about, you will be able to figure out what needs to be done to move toward your ideal working life—and to create an action plan that allows you to spend your time and energy on things that bring you fulfillment and happiness.

You should spend most of your time with people who enable you, who give you energy, and who help you grow and develop.

---

6   *Manage your relationships.* Essential for living a fulfilled life is to be selective about your relationships. As I have said repeatedly, *Homo sapiens* is above all a social being, hardwired for connection. However, you should be selective about these connections and develop relationships with people who energize you. In the same vein, you should let go of relationships that drain you of energy, such as with negative people, dishonest people, people who don't respect you, people who are overly critical, and people who prevent your further development. In addition, you should keep in mind that hanging on to relationships for selfish reasons will not give you love, fulfillment, or inner happiness. Of course, in the context of social connections, the most important relationship to look for is one with a compatible partner. Finding such a person will make a world of difference to living a fulfilled life. Thus, when all is said and done, you should spend most of your time with people who enable you, who give you energy, and who help you grow and develop.

Homo sapiens is above all a social being, hardwired for connection.

---

7   *Keep on learning.* An important part of living a fulfilling life is to keep on learning. The whole of life, from the moment you are born to the moment you die, can be a process of continuous learning. Therefore, you should have an attitude toward life that there is always something new to learn. Doing so

enables you to tell a story of hope. Impress on yourself that the moment you stop learning you're dead.

Impress on yourself that the moment you stop learning you're dead.

To be a good learner, however, you will need to get out of your comfort zone, embrace new ideas, and try new things. Your mind, unlike your body, can continue to grow as you continue to live. If you keep on learning, you will never cease to develop as the world is a laboratory to the inquiring mind. Remember that there is something to learn from *everything* you see, hear, and experience. And the beautiful thing about learning is that nobody can take it away from you.

The whole of life, from the moment you are born to the moment you die, can be a process of continuous learning.

---

8   *Practice gratitude.* Practicing gratitude makes you feel better. To lead a fulfilling life, you should acknowledge the good that you have in your life. After all, people who live the most fulfilling lives are those who experience gratitude for what they have. And, what's more, experiencing these feelings of gratitude also implies letting the people who've touched you know about your gratitude toward them. If you don't tell them, they'll never know. But when you do so, there are great benefits to expressing gratitude, including improved relationships, better physical and emotional health, healthier sleep habits, greater mental stamina, more energy, and greater overall happiness.[1] Being grateful is one of the simplest and most powerful things you can do to live a full and happy life.

9   *Consult a guide.* In this journey (as was suggested for some of the other people mentioned in this book), it can be helpful to have coaches or psychotherapists to guide you toward a more fulfilling life. These people can provide you with a modicum of safety and perspective as you explore your inner world. After all, your head can be an unsafe neighborhood where

you would be wise not to go alone. Aided by helping professionals, however, you may be able to see yourself in the mirror in a very different way. In fact, there's no faster way to work on yourself than to have someone else work with you, guiding you to understand yourself better. Coaches and psychotherapists help you to "wake up" and become more mindful of your daily activities and patterns of behavior. They share important insights and advice that you can use to improve yourself. They will challenge your fears, unlock your potential, and help you move forward. With their assistance you may also come to understand what's holding you back, a knowledge that will help you to set yourself free. In fact, helping professionals can do for the rest of your life what personal trainers can do for your health and fitness. They guide you to experience the deepest feelings of personal worth, purpose, and richness in living.

10   *Living to give.* Finally, an important aspect of living a fulfilling life is to make a contribution to improving the world. Sooner or later, a life directed chiefly toward the fulfillment of personal desires will always lead to bitter disappointment. Important to living the good life is therefore to take responsibility for the happiness of other living beings as well as your own. In other words, true fulfillment doesn't mean living to get, but living to give. And while you're doing things for a greater cause, never forget that giving also has many beneficial effects, physiologically and mentally. For example, it has been shown that giving to others lowers your blood pressure, increases your sense of self-esteem, improves your happiness, and even helps you live longer.[2] And isn't that a good reason for making the meaning of the universe part of the meaning of your own life?

Important to living the good life is therefore to take responsibility for the happiness of other living beings as well as your own.

In the context of living a fulfilling life, it is death that gives a perspective on the value of your life. By imagining your own nonexistence, you get a sense of what is most important about your own life. Thus, while you are living, focus on what *truly* gives you meaning. Don't get fixated on achieving status, fame, wealth, or material possessions. These are all symbols of impermanence. Ultimately, they will become irrelevant the day you die. What does survive, however, is your legacy. *What would you like people to say about you? What are the stories about you that you would like to be passed on when you're gone? How can you work toward writing those stories today?*

Now, returning to Philip, who wanted to have a life, hopefully he will have the courage to begin this journey. And he should start it today. Today could be the day to let go of what's holding him back. Today could be the day to begin creating a fulfilling life. He shouldn't just wait for life to happen. To quote Robert Louis Stevenson, "To be what we are, and to become what we are capable of becoming, is the only end of life."[3] It is high time for Philip to be able to tell a different story about himself.

In the context of living a fulfilling life, it is death that gives a perspective on the value of your life.

NOTES

[1] Nicole McDermott (2023). "The Mental Health Benefits of Gratitude." *Forbes*, 10 November.

[2] "Why Giving Is Good for Your Health." Cleveland Clinic, 6 December 2022. https://health.clevelandclinic.org/why-giving-is-good-for-your-health

[3] Robert Louis Stevenson (1882). *Familiar Studies of Men and Books*. London: Chatto and Windus, p. 164.

CONCLUDING COMMENTS

Paris, ... evil-hearted Paris, fair to see, but woman-mad, and false of tongue, would that you had never been born, or that you had died unwed. Better so, than live to be disgraced and looked askance at. Will not the Achaeans mock at us and say that we have sent one to champion us who is fair to see but who has neither wit nor courage?

—Homer

Storytelling has been the major theme of this book. As I have mentioned repeatedly, the stories we hold in common are an important part of the ties that bind people, cultures, and nations together. Clearly, stories are the vehicle you use to make sense of your life in a world that often defies logic. Given the effects of neural mirroring, when stories are being told, for both tellers and listeners the narratives that emerge can be looked at as a form of mental time travel, enabling the re-enactment of episodic memories of self and others. Clearly, the tales you tell hold a powerful sway over your memories, behaviors, and even your identity. When you are captivated by the stories you listen to—helped by your imagination—you will be able to transcend time and space. And, as you may also have

DOI: 10.4324/9781003508939-13

discovered by now, stories contain multiple meanings, having the power to convey complex ideas in a more understandable way. In addition, stories will help you to explore your identity and discover what you are made of. In fact, the life story can be a vehicle for grappling with the essential question: *Who am I?*

Stories are the vehicle you use to make sense of your life in a world that often defies logic.

THE TRAGIC TRANSIENCE OF THINGS

With respect to identity, you may have come to realize that who you are is shaped by the tales you remember of your childhood experiences. Eventually, as you move through the various stages of life, your identity will become more coherent. Gradually, if you're able to successfully surmount life's challenges, guided by your life story you will discover unity and purpose. And you will discover that your personal story has the power to tie together your life's past, present, and future. Through your personal story, you will acquire a sense of continuity and sameness across situations and over time. In that respect, storytelling is ultimately a creative act of pattern recognition. Yet, it is also a retrospective reconstruction of meaningful life events. As a storyteller, helped by the characters that you will put into the scene, and through the plots and settings that you have created, you're trying to make previously invisible truths visible. In fact, when you tell your story, you put into people's imagination a series of dots that they're challenged to connect. It will be your way to have them make sense of what you have become.

Your personal story has the power to tie together your life's past, present, and future.

Clearly, the various existing "talking cures," especially psychoanalysis, have taken advantage of the human need to tell stories, particularly our own. These clinical interventions have always been endeavors whereby individuals have the opportunity to replay and reinterpret their life stories. And it may be a truism to say that we are as healthy and as confident as the stories we're able to tell ourselves. If we can articulate our life's story constructively, it creates a sense of agency. Doing so will be an antidote to helplessness. Clearly, being able to tell our story in a cohesive manner is a great way to disarm the demons that dwell inside us. Resilience relies in part on this kind of autobiographical storytelling, explaining how we have been able to navigate life's challenges.

My hope is that you, the reader of this book, while trying to make sense of the various stories contained here, will come to understand the extent to which the stories you tell yourself have influenced the way you are. Reading the essays in this book, you may come to realize how much you have been living within a web of stories, and so start to understand better the world you're living in. As an illustration, think about how religious stories may have taught you the fundamentals of religion and rules of conduct. Think of the fables and parables that have molded your values. And reflect on how stories about your national, cultural, or family history have shaped your attitudes about yourself and others. Stories will tell you what you once knew and forgot, but may also remind you of what you have not yet imagined.

It may be a truism to say that we are as healthy and as confident as the stories we're able to tell ourselves.

What I have also tried to point out in this book is our hunger for stories, the degree to which storytelling is part of our very being. Storytelling is also a form of history, making for a modicum of immortality. Most of us have experienced how storytelling passes from one generation to another; how telling and listening to stories can be a bonding ritual that breaks through illusions of separateness, creating a deep sense of collective interdependence.

By having read this book, I hope you will have become a better storyteller. Knowing what you know now, you may have become more attuned to the many layers hidden within these stories. In addition, I have tried to expose the reader to more troubled tales dealing with various forms of personality dysfunction. My wish is that by reading these tales, you will have gained greater insight about your own life story and, as a result, you may be better equipped to interpret your own life as an ongoing story. You may come to understand how your life story has shaped you as an individual.

Stories will tell you of what you once knew and forgot, but also may remind you of what you have not yet imagined.

THE TALE OF A BEAUTY CONTEST WITH A "CATCH"

As must have become clear by now, the purpose of a storyteller is not to tell you how to think but to give you questions to think about. To continue this process, I will end this book with another tale that may provoke your thinking. I am referring to a very famous narrative, which like all the others that have been told, incorporates a number of explicit and implicit messages. It is a tale that has had a great influence on Western civilization. In this instance, it is a tale that superficially refers to a beauty contest. But there is much more to it than meets the eye. In fact, if you consider its cultural relevance, it can be considered the "mother" of all beauty contests. And even though beauty contests often lead to arguments among competitors and spectators, the stakes in this particular beauty contest appeared to have been so much higher. In this instance, the person who was asked to judge was faced with choices pertaining to some of the most important drivers of human nature. However, given the momentousness of the decision that needed to be made, whatever the choice was going to be, the consequences were going to be dramatic. In fact, as the story points out, depending on the choice, the outcome of this beauty contest could cause war, destruction, and death.

I am referring to "The Judgment of Paris." This famous contest described in Greek mythology (as presented in the *Iliad*, the ancient Greek epic poem written by Homer) was the event that set the stage for the Trojan War. And the choice that was made would lead to the ultimate destruction of Troy. As can be expected, by presenting this narrative, Homer was describing a cautionary tale, telling his listeners "be careful what you wish for." However, in his efforts at storytelling, he wasn't very explicit about the messages contained in this narrative. Still, by drawing on a pantheon of gods and goddesses—including their symbolic representations—he was asking the listeners to draw their own conclusions about what he implied. However, the essence of the tale was to challenge people, to ask them what they would have done if they had been tasked to be the judge. How would they have dealt with this human dilemma?

Storytelling is also a form of history, making for a modicum of immortality.

As a story, "The Judgment of Paris" has influenced Western culture to an impressive extent. Philosophers, art historians, and psychologists have pondered on this dilemma. Painters, in particular, have been enamored of this story, allowing some of the most renowned not only to portray the consequences of love and passion but also their ideal of female beauty. Here, we can't help but think that the cause for the popularity of this subject, and one of the reasons that so many artists produced their version of this event, is that it also presented an opportunity to produce female nudes of an undoubtedly erotic nature—and of course an opportunity for their clients to enjoy looking at this imagery.

But let us get back to the story. It all began with the marriage of King Peleus to the sea nymph Thetis. As this was a very significant event, all the gods and goddesses were asked to come to the celebration. For obvious reasons, however, Eris, the goddess of strife and discord, was not invited. After all, wherever she went, she always spewed hatred and started fights. Sadly, however, the unwillingness of the gods to invite her to the party would have unexpected consequences. Ironically, instead of avoiding strife, it would lead to unimaginable strife taking place across the whole known Greek world.

When Eris heard about the festivities, she decided to make an appearance anyway but in an invisible form. Ill-tempered for not being invited—and wanting to ruin the happy occasion—she decided to bring a gift of a golden apple, meant to be given to the fairest person there. Three goddesses claimed the golden apple: Hera, the goddess of marriage (and also the wife of Zeus), Athena, the goddess of wisdom and warfare (Zeus's daughter), and Aphrodite, the goddess of love and beauty. Interestingly enough, no males volunteered as candidates.

Naturally, Zeus, the king of all the gods, was expected to make the choice. But he thought better of it. He did not want to upset any of the three goddesses. After all, choosing between his wife and his daughter would have been very awkward and, given his extensive history of infidelities, not choosing Hera would lead to even more marital discord. Instead, he suggested that someone else should be chosen to make a fair choice. So, Zeus told the gathering that a mortal man who had recently shown his exemplary fairness in another contest would be the most suitable arbitrator. He was referring to Paris, who was living as a shepherd on the mountains near Troy, unaware that he was the son of Troy's King Priam.

According to the story, following Zeus' recommendation, the messenger god Hermes brought the three contenders before the surprised Paris. After informing him of Zeus' will, the young, inexperienced Paris looked at the three goddesses but found it difficult to decide. To persuade him of their case, the three goddesses stripped nude to convince the mortal prince of their beauty. While Paris was having another look at them, each one of the goddesses also offered him a "gift." They were trying to bribe him in making his choice, presenting him with an offer he wouldn't be able to refuse. Hera offered Paris power. She promised that, if he chose her, he would receive untold wealth and would be in charge of all the realms of the ancient world. Athena went next. She offered him not only great wisdom but that she would also make him the greatest warrior of all time, never to be defeated in battle. Aphrodite seduced him with love, telling him that she would get him the most beautiful female mortal in the world.

Of course, none of the three goddesses told Paris that their gifts could have extremely serious consequences. Although Hera could make Paris the ruler of Europe and Asia, she didn't tell him that so much power would bring grave repercussions. Athena's offer to make Paris the greatest warrior in the world would have meant wars in which many people would die even though he would win. Finally, Aphrodite forgot to mention that the most beautiful woman in the world was already married.

As we know from the myth, Paris, after careful consideration, presented the golden apple to Aphrodite, without giving any thought to the consequences. He didn't think about how the two goddesses he rejected would react to his choice. Their abiding animosity would later be displayed during the Trojan War when both goddesses sided with the Achaean (Greek) forces (although Aphrodite would try to assist the Trojans).

Was the point made in the story that, given human nature, it was to be expected that for mere mortals the sexual drive would over-rule everything else? Why didn't Paris reflect on the consequences of his choice? And why didn't he pay sufficient attention to the offers of Hera and Athena?

After he had made his choice, Aphrodite revealed that Helen, the wife of Menelaus, the King of Sparta, was the most beautiful woman in the world. This little hiccup notwithstanding, Aphrodite delivered to Paris what she promised. But muddleheaded as she seemed to be, she also didn't seem to have thought through the consequences of her choice.

After having claimed his rightful position as a prince of Troy, Paris set sail for Sparta, to arrive at the palace of Menelaus with rich gifts. Predictably, helped by Aphrodite, Paris persuaded Helen to follow him to Troy. The story doesn't make clear, however, whether she was persuaded or abducted. Yet, her move to Troy resulted in the most epic war of that day and age, the Trojan War—a conflict that lasted for ten years.

Stories of the gods always exist in part to provide moral lessons and commentary on human behavior. The story of "The Judgment of Paris" allows the reader to decide what's most important when reflecting on the decisions you are asked to make. Will you follow Aphrodite's passions, Hera's family duties, or Athena's wisdom? Clearly, putting yourself in Paris' shoes, he was faced with a conundrum. His predicament was a Faustian one. Whatever choice he made would have dire consequences. Whomever he chose, strife would follow. But could he have acted differently?

From a rational point of view, Paris should have chosen Hera. If he had given the matter more thought, she was really the most powerful goddess. Although Athena would give him wisdom and Aphrodite was prepared to give him the most beautiful woman, Hera offered power. Also, her influence and rage were far more deadly than those of Athena and Aphrodite. Even though Hera did not always use her powers to their full extent, nobody would want to cross her. Even the king of the gods, Zeus, seemed to be scared of her, so perhaps Paris should have been too.

Naturally, if Paris had selected her, Hera would have been very pleased. He should have realized that having her on his side would have been a great boon. Also, from what we know about her, she was loyal to a fault. Despite all of Zeus' amorous adventures, she still put up with him and she would always help those whom she deemed worthy. Consequently, if Paris could get on her good side, even if he made a lot of enemies (including powerful ones like Athena and Aphrodite), with Hera's protection, they would leave him alone. In other words, although the two other goddesses might curse him for not choosing them, Hera would thwart any attempt. In addition, what made the choice of Hera even more attractive was her offer to make him the ruler of Europe and Asia—the realms of the ancient world.

It must have thus been obvious that the offers of the other two goddesses weren't in the same league. Although the offers of wisdom or being made a great warrior were not to be sniffed at, in the long run power would be of more use. Granted, if Paris had chosen Athena, he might still have become a formidable and renowned man, wealthy and admired. However, it was risky to cross Hera. Of course, with Aphrodite against him, he would never have found love. Also, a factor that should be kept in mind is that, if he had chosen Hera, Athena—wise as she was—didn't seem to be a goddess who tended to hold grudges. Furthermore, Aphrodite was not the most reliable person, and was not known for her great planning, as her choice of Helen illustrated. Eventually, her spell on Helen wore off. Helen went back to her husband and, effectively, Paris ended up with nothing.

Of course, Paris may have picked Aphrodite because she really was the most beautiful of the three goddesses. Still, was his mind completely clear? His lonely existence in the mountains may have gotten to him. It may have stimulated his sex drive, explaining why an affair with the most beautiful woman on Earth became his preference. Unfortunately, it looked like he allowed his sex drive to take his brain hostage. Yet, it could very well be that Helen really was so beautiful that even being able to be her husband for a day was more appealing than conquering or possessing the whole world.

If Paris had been an out-of-the-box thinker, he could have made a paradoxical intervention. What if he had said that Eris, the goddess of strife and discord, who as he might have overheard was the source of all this trouble, was the most beautiful one? If he had done so, he might have foiled her spiteful scheme. Even though it would have made her angry, most likely he would have had all the other gods on his side. They would have been quite amused to see her angry. Or, to reflect on another outcome, naively she might take it as a compliment if he had chosen her. If so, it would have been very well possible that the whole affair would have fizzled out.

What Paris also could have done, as another out-of-the-box intervention, was to have the three goddesses swear that, whatever choice he made, it would have no negative consequences for him or his loved ones. If they refused, he could have expressed his unwillingness to choose any of them. For example, he could have said that all of them were so beautiful that he couldn't make up his mind. Hopefully, Paris would get away with this response without being punished by Zeus for refusing his orders.

THE CALL OF THE UNCONSCIOUS

Of course, the reason I present yet another story is to stimulate the reader's curiosity about the various conscious and unconscious messages contained in this narrative. And, as I mentioned before, the power of storytelling is to transmit messages, often of a moral nature. But in understanding these messages, Paris failed miserably. As the story makes clear, Paris didn't display the common sense needed to be an effective judge in this beauty contest. He didn't "listen with the third ear." He didn't seem to have any "night vision," that is, the ability to pay attention to the underlying messages that were part of the decision he was asked to make. Accordingly, he didn't realize the consequences of his decision.

However, despite all the possible alternatives, it remains debatable whether a better decision, devoid of bribes, would have avoided these negative future events. After all, it was said that the Trojan War had been an event planned by Zeus. A prophecy had been made at Paris' birth that the newborn would bring about the destruction of Troy. Apparently, events had been preordained long before "The Judgment of Paris."

That being said, the tale of "The Judgment of Paris" has retained its relevance because, like all other myths, it taps into primary human themes of human behavior such as sex, infidelity, male and female power, male stupidity, hubris, greed, jealousy, and envy, themes that still resonate thousands of years later. After all, it is these themes that often cause the downfall of human beings.

Still, when all is said and done, the main moral message of this narrative remains. What to choose: family values (Hera), wisdom (Athena), or sexuality (Aphrodite)? Since the beginning of time, human beings have had to deal with these major themes. And when these three themes come into play, you should be careful what you wish for. You should be aware of the consequences of impulsive actions. Like Paris, you may want to resort to the quick fix. But quick fixes are rarely long lasting. To prevent disasters from happening, he should perhaps have resorted to an ancient Greek proverb, "Know thyself," because to lead a well-lived life, it is important to acquire self-knowledge and self-awareness. You should not be tempted to become hubristic. Furthermore, a modern-day Paris should perhaps pay attention to the warning of the philosopher and naturalist Henry David Thoreau: "The question is not what you look at, but what you see."[1]

Wisdom cannot be rushed. It comes in its own time. It lives inside all of us, if you are quiet enough to listen for it. It is a byproduct of simply living.

In Greek philosophy, there is also the maxim, "moderation in all things." Paris should have realized that what the three goddesses offered him as "gifts" were offers that weren't very moderate. And as the myth makes quite clear, excess in any of the choices would contribute to very unexpected outcomes. In reading this book you have hopefully learned that becoming a better storyteller and story listener may help you to choose wisely. However, you may also have learned that wisdom cannot be rushed. It comes in its own time. It lives inside all of us, if you are quiet enough to hear it. It is a byproduct of simply living. Thus, knowing that stories can pack so much power, you need to seed them with wisdom.

To sum up, the art of storytelling is not only for you. It is also your obligation to be able to tell stories for the next generation. This will be the way to create human continuity. This is the way to fight oblivion. Storytelling is the most powerful way to put ideas out into the world. Stories make you think and feel; stories transport you to other places; and stories inspire change. Therefore, if you want to change what is happening in the world you're living in, you'd better make an effort to start with changing your own story.

It is your obligation to be able to tell stories for the next generation.

NOTE

[1] Henry David Thoreau (1851). "Journal II, 1850–September 15, 1851." In Bradford Torrey (ed.), *The Writings of Henry David Thoreau, Vol. 8*. Boston, MA and New York: Houghton Mifflin.

Epigraph sources

INTRODUCTION

Molière (2008 [1668]). *Amphitryon*. Act II, Scene III. Translated by A. R. Waller. Project Gutenberg. Available at: https://www.gutenberg.org/files/2536/2536-h/2536-h.htm

Lewis Carroll (1865). *Alice's Adventures in Wonderland*. London: Macmillan.

CHAPTER 1

R. Campbell Thompson (trans.) (1928). *The Epic of Gilgamesh*. London: Luzac & Co.

CHAPTER 2

George Bernard Shaw (1944). "Creed and Conduct." In *Everybody's Political What's What?* London: Constable and Company, p. 133.

Charles Dickens (1894 [1861]). *Great Expectations*. London: Chapman & Hall, p. 366.

CHAPTER 3

Leo Tolstoy (1899). *Resurrection*. Book 1, Chapter LVIX. First English edition, 1900. London: Frances Riddell Henderson.

CHAPTER 4

Abraham Lincoln (1889 [1842]). *An Address Delivered by Abraham Lincoln, before the Springfield Washingtonian Temperance Society, at the Second Presbyterian Church, Springfield, Illinois, on the 22d Day of February, 1842*. Springfield, IL: O. H. Oldroyd.

Rudyard Kipling (1909). "Wressley of the Foreign Office." In *Plain Tales from the Hills*. New York: Nottingham Society.

Kenneth Grahame (1913 [1908]). *The Wind in the Willows*. New York: Charles Scribner's Sons.

CHAPTER 5

Ralph Waldo Emerson (1890 [1838]). "Literary Ethics." Address to the Literary Societies of Dartmouth College, 24 July 1838. New York: Thomas Y. Crowell & Co.

Rainer Maria Rilke (1932 [1929]). *Briefe an einen jungen Dichter*. [Letters to a Young Poet.] Leipzig: Insel Verlag. Author's translation.

CHAPTER 6

Marcus Aurelius (1910 [c. AD 121–180]). *The Meditations of Marcus Aurelius*. Book x.16. Translated by George Long. London: Blackie & Son.

André Gide (1927 [1925]). *The Counterfeiters*. Translated by Dorothy Bussy. New York: Alfred A. Knopf.

Lau-Tsze (1868 [sixth century BC]). *The Speculations on Metaphysics, Polity, and Morality, of "the Old Philospher," Lau-Tsze*. Translated by John Chalmers. London: Trübner & Co, Chapter XXXIII.

CHAPTER 7

Arthur Schopenhauer (1887 [1818]). *The World as Will and Idea*. Translated by R. B. Haldane and J. Kemp. Boston, MA: Ticknor and Company, Volume II.

Johann Peter Eckermann (1850). *Conversations of Goethe with Eckermann and Soret*. Translated by John Oxenford. London: Smith, Elder, and Co. Originally published in German, 1836–1848.

Franz Kafka (1925). *Der Prozess*. [The Trial.] Germany: Verlag die Schmiede. Author's translation.

CHAPTER 8

Alexander Berkman (1912). *Prison Memoirs of an Anarchist*. New York: Mother Earth Publishing Association.

Thomas Carlyle (1841). "Lecture III: The Hero as Poet." In *On Heroes, Hero-Worship, & the Heroic in History*. London: James Fraser.

CHAPTER 9

Friedrich Nietzsche (1889). *Götzen-Dämmerung, oder wie man mit dem Hammer philosophirt*. [The Twilight of the Idols, or how to philosophise with a hammer.] Leipzig: Verlag Von C. G. Neumann. Author's translation.

Benjamin Disraeli (1880). *Endymion*, vol 2. London: Longmans, Green, and Co.

Plutarch (1693 [c. second century AD]). *Plutarch's Lives Volume III: Q. Sertorius. Translated from the Greek by Several Hands*. London: Jacob Tonson.

CHAPTER 10

Merle Johnson (ed.). (1927). *More Maxims of Mark*. Privately printed.

Niccolò Machiavelli (1883 [1517]). *Discourses on the First Decade of Titus Livius*. Translated by Ninian Hill. London: Kegan Paul, Trench & Co.

CHAPTER 11

Leo Tolstoy (1899 [1878]). *Anna Karenina*. Translated by Nathan Haskell Dole. New York: Thomas Y. Crowell & Co. [Passage in German.]

Sigmund Freud (1963 [1908]). "'Civilized' Sexual Morality and Modern Nervousness." In *Sexuality and the Psychology of Love*. New York: Simon & Schuster, p. 25.

D. H. Lawrence (1932). *Lady Chatterley's Lover*. London: Martin Secker.

CHAPTER 12

Gilbert K. Chesterton (1905). *Heretics*. London: Bodley Head, p. 31.

Marcus Aurelius (1910 [c. AD 121–180]). *The Meditations of Marcus Aurelius*. Book vii.61. Translated by George Long. London: Blackie & Son.

Arthur Schopenhauer (1902 [1851]). "On Noise." In *Studies in Pessimism*. Translated by T. Bailey Saunders. New York: A. L. Burt Co.

CONCLUDING COMMENTS

Homer (1898 [c. eighth century BC]). *The Iliad of Homer*. Translated by Samuel Butler. London: Longmans, Green, and Co.

Index

Printed in the United States
by Baker & Taylor Publisher Services